C. F. Peter Collingridge

The civil principality

C. F. Peter Collingridge

The civil principality

ISBN/EAN: 9783741155901

Manufactured in Europe, USA, Canada, Australia, Japa

Cover: Foto ©Thomas Meinert / pixelio.de

Manufactured and distributed by brebook publishing software
(www.brebook.com)

C. F. Peter Collingridge

The civil principality

"THEN THE PONTIFFS ARE FREE."

THE CIVIL PRINCIPALITY

OF

THE VICAR OF CHRIST REVEALED IN THE HOLY SCRIPTURES.

AN APPEAL TO THE CLERGY AND TO ALL FRIENDS OF THE HOLY SEE.

BY THE
Rev. C. F. PETER COLLINGRIDGE

" Dabit illi Dominus Deus sedem David patris ejus et regnabit in domo Jacob in æternum."

THIS DISCOURSE, FULL OF ASSOCIATION WITH HIM,
IS INSCRIBED
TO THE MEMORY OF ALFRED,
A DEAR BROTHER,
WHO HAVING OFFERED TO GOD FOR SERVICE IN THE SANCTUARY
A HEART ADMIRABLE FOR PURITY, DETACHMENT, AND
CONFORMITY TO THE DIVINE WILL,
VOLUNTEERED IN A TIME OF DANGER FOR THE
DEFENCE OF THE PRINCELY RIGHTS OF THE VICAR OF CHRIST,
FIRMLY RESOLVING
THAT SHOULD NO SACRIFICE OF BLOOD BE REQUIRED,
HIS FIRST OBLATION SHOULD BE CONSUMMATED.
THE SACRIFICE
IN THE CAUSE OF THE HOLY SEE WAS ACCEPTED.
HE DIED OF HIS WOUNDS AT NEROLA,
OCTOBER 18TH, 1867.

L. J. C.

INTRODUCTION.

DIVINE PROVIDENCE, which maintains the order of the universe, extends to the physical world, to the moral world, and to the supernatural world. We are taught by the words of the late Pope Pius IX., and by the declaration of the Bishops of the world assembled around him in 1862 (see Appendix) that the Roman Pontiff obtained the Civil Principality by a peculiar design of Divine Providence, and that the temporal sovereignty did not accrue to him by the effect of hazard, but was granted to him by a special disposition of God. Such is the grave and authentic teaching of the Church of God, which deserves the greatest attention at the present day. The measured terms of the Pontifical utterance and of the Bishop's declaration are very striking ; but, what is more so, is the vast import of that conjoint teaching and its infolded character.

Twenty-nine years have elapsed since the Church raised her voice in that solemn manner, during which long period we have been schooled by the sad lesson of events. Is it presumptuous to inquire whether, if there be any analogy between the Civil Principality of the Vicar of Christ and other points of Catholic doctrine, which have at last been put into a clear light, we may not legitimately expect a further elucidation of this teaching.

1. Are we to understand by the solemn teaching of the Church in 1862 that a peculiar design or ruling of Divine Providence raises the Civil Principality above the ordinary moral order of society, and transfers it to the supernatural order ? Or are we free to hold that, in spite of such " particular design of Divine Providence," and " special disposition of God," the Civil Principality remains subject to the natural laws which govern the moral world, and hence to the ebb and flow of the affairs of men ?

2. Are we to understand that the Civil Principality is something less than a direct gift of God ?

3. If so, is the Civil Principality then first founded on a mere human right, springing from cession, gift, or growth of favouring circumstances ?

4. Could any divine sanction, bestowed after the foundation of the Church, on a mere human institution, change its nature ?

5. Are we taught that the Civil Principality is inalienable under all possible circumstances ?

6. Is sovereign power founded on mere human right inalienable under all possible circumstances ?

7. Are we taught that the Civil Principality is a right inherent to the office of the Vicar of Christ, or may we hold that it is adventitious?

8. When we are taught that the temporal sovereignty was not added to the Holy See by an effect of hazard, but was granted by a special disposition of God, are we to understand that the Roman Pontiff's right did not arise from human activity or natural causation, but is founded on God's own gift and institution?

9. Can an absolutely inalienable sovereign right have any other than a divine foundation?

10. Is it conceivable that the Civil Principality should be inherent to the office of the Vicar of Christ, and thus constitute an inalienable temporal right without a distinctly divine foundation?

11. Supposing the spiritual and universal supremacy of the Roman Pontiff necessarily implies a *de jure* inalienable temporal sovereignty, is it conceivable that God failed to grant such a right from the beginning?

12. If the existence of the Roman Pontiff's temporal right may be inferred from the necessity of the temporal power, should not the basis of that right be discoverable?

13. Which is more conducive to the interests of the Faith, and to those of the Church, merely to infer the existence of the Pontiff's temporal right, or to discover it plainly by indicating its foundation?

14. In what sense does the Civil Principality belong to the Catholic world? How, when, and from whom did Christians acquire that right?

15. The territory over which any sovereignty is exercised must be determinable, because no territory is geographically indeterminable. Therefore the "temporal possessions" of the Roman Pontiff must be determinable as to extent. By what standard are we to judge of such extent?

16. If the gift of temporal sovereignty to the Roman Pontiff be divine, it was contemporaneous with the foundation of the Church. For the Divine plan was then complete, and nothing has been added to it since. On what occasion, then, was the gift bestowed?

17. Should we be afraid to invoke more light on this subject, or is it a matter of indifference to acquire a more definite idea of the Civil Principality?

May we not legitimately inquire concerning the bestowal of temporal power on the Roman Pontiff: "*Quis, quid, ubi, quibus auxiliis, cur, quomodo, quando?*"

These are questions which I have feebly attempted to solve in this little work, which was published from the beginning with a practical object in view. It can possess no claim save to invite the clergy and all friends of the Holy See to a closer study of the foundation of the temporal power of the Pope, in the hope that not mere secular loyalty will be encouraged towards the Pontiff-king, but that a more sublime and potent feeling may be appealed to, namely, our Faith. For "this is the victory which overcometh the world, our Faith."

C. F. P. C.

ST. JAMES'S, COLCHESTER,

November 3rd, 1890.

Dear Father Collingridge,

I have read your paper upon the Temporal Power of the Holy See with much interest. I recommend you to publish it. The subject has been abundantly treated from the historical, the political, and the economic points of view, as it regards the interests of Christendom. It has not however been so fully brought before the public from the scriptural and theological standpoint. You have attempted to analyse and draw out the meaning which lies hidden in the words of Sacred Scripture and in events recorded in the Gospel. Thus your study cannot fail to interest a great number of Catholic minds. The more you can show that the Prerogatives of the Roman Pontiff are in reality inherited from Blessed Peter, who in his turn received them from His Divine Master upon being associated with Him as His Vicar and Representative on earth, the more you will raise the esteem in which those Prerogatives are held by Catholics.

The principal text on which you comment—that of Matthew xvii. 25, 26—is carefully examined by Suarez in his "Defence of the Faith against Anglican Errors," where he asks the question, Why does Christ associate Peter with Himself in the freedom of the children of kings and in the payment of the stater?

This great theologian, who speaks for the whole school, says that Christ declared Peter to be exempt from tribute just as He Himself was ; and that we are to understand that Christ granted this privilege of exemption to Peter because Peter was to be the Prince and Head of the Church and the Vicar of Jesus Christ Himself.

This privilege was therefore not *personal* to Peter alone, but *real*, and attached to the dignity and office which passes on to his successors in virtue of Divine power and of the peculiar institution and will of Christ. If tribute be the sign of temporal dependence and subjection, he who is not really subject to the payment of tribute is not really under temporal subjection. He is independent : if independent he is Sovereign. The principle, therefore, of the temporal independence of the Pope appears to be contained in the text of the Gospel just referred to.

That there may be, and are, differences of opinion among theologians as to the precise meaning of certain texts and facts, is no reason why we should not put forward for acceptance the sense and the consequences which we, after careful study of such texts or facts, consider to be evidently contained in them.

This you have done with becoming modesty, and I therefore think that your little treatise cannot fail to render a real service to the great cause of the Papacy.

Wishing you every blessing,

I am, your faithful and devoted servant,

✠ HERBERT,
BISHOP OF SALFORD.

THE CIVIL PRINCIPALITY OR TEMPORAL PRINCEDOM OF THE VICAR OF CHRIST, FORESHADOWED IN THE OLD TESTAMENT AND VINDICATED IN THE NEW.

" Then the children are free."—St. Matthew xvii.

Dear Brethren,—I have frequently in past discourses reminded you of the event which took place in Rome on the 20th of September of the year 1870, of which I was an eye-witness ; how the Vicar of Christ was then violently despoiled of the last remnant of territorial independence constituting what is called the Civil Principality. I have quoted the page of history in proof that the Civil Principality was acknowledged as a right of the successors of Peter so soon as rulers and subjects embracing the Christian Faith understood the unique, supreme, and universal position of the Vicar of Our Lord, and that in all Christian ages both Kings and their subjects have in their conduct towards the Pontiffs, more eloquently than in words, manifested their implicit Faith in his civil independence and temporal sovereignty.

I have now to inquire whether this great historical fact which, like a ray of Heavenly guidance, is cast down the Christian ages with only here and there an exceptional diminution of splendour, is merely the outcome of the goodwill of Christian nations, or a provisional state allowed by Divine Providence to be followed by some more enlightened agreement with modern rulers of the Nineteenth Century, or whether it is not rather the work of the Invisible Head of the Church, securing to His Vicar the exercise of a right once Divinely bestowed upon Him in the person of Peter. If once we become convinced that his Civil Principality or Temporal Princedom is a gift of Jesus Christ and an essential part of the Divine Plan for the Church Militant, we shall not be surprised, as unbelievers have sometimes been, at the luminous fact just alluded to, namely : that except in times of persecution, which God's providence over His Church does not permit to last long, the Roman Pontiffs have ever enjoyed territorial independence with all Kingly rights. I maintain then that *the Civil Principality or Temporal Princedom is a gift of Jesus Christ, and a Divine institution foreshadowed in the Old Testament and vindicated in the New.* To defend this thesis, dear brethren, I will confine myself to texts that are clear in themselves or susceptible of plain deductions, and shall have recourse to two principal arguments.

First : That the order of Christ, which is that of Melchisedech, to which the Roman Pontiffs belong, constitutes them Kings and therefore gives them a territorial independence.

Second : That the Roman Pontiffs were actually associated in the person of Peter in the supreme independence of the Son of Man, and therefore in His earthly Freedom.

I.—That the order of Christ, which is that of Melchisedech, to which the Roman Pontiffs belong, constitutes them Kings and therefore gives them a territorial independence.

THE ORDER OF MELCHISEDECH.

Let us examine the essential features of the order of Melchisedech by which it is distinguished from the Levitical order. We read in Genesis, chapter xiv., that " Melchisedech, the King of Salem, bringing forth bread and wine, for he was a priest of the most High God, blessed " Abraham. In the Psalms we read the following words of King David in reference to his Divine descendant and successor : " Thou art a priest for ever according to the order of Melchisedech." These words are quoted in the Epistle to the Hebrews. From the commentary of St. Paul and from the tradition of the Church we gather these essential features of the new · order which distinguish it from the old.

1. That it is the fulfilment of the old which it abolishes.
2. That the Pontiff thereof belongs to no particular tribe.

3. That his oblation is that of bread and wine.
4. That besides being priest he is King.

Each of these essential features must now come under our particular notice :—

First : The first feature or characteristic of the order of Melchisedech seems also to be the one which the Apostle St. Paul writing from Italy insists on principally. For the Hebrews clung to the old order of things. If the Levitical order were changed, then the law, then the inheritance of the sceptre, then the whole national organization must be at least altered. St. Paul insisted that the new order put an end to the old, that Christ constituted "priest for ever according to the order of Melchisedech" had entered the true sanctuary, Heaven, which He had opened not with the blood of animals, but with His own, and once for all ; that the typical sanctuary of the temple, with the annual visit of the Pontiff carrying the typical blood was therefore put an end to.

Again according to the Apostle, Melchisedech had by legal prescription neither "beginning of days nor end of life" which was typical of the eternal priesthood of Christ, whereas the Jewish Pontiff had a limited term of office, which was ominous of the limited duration of the Levitical order.

Second : The second essential feature of the order of Melchisedech which distinguishes it from the order of Aaron consists in this, that the Pontiff thereof belongs to no particular tribe, but may be chosen from any nation, whereas the Jewish Pontiff was taken from the tribe of Levi and the family of Aaron. Which St. Paul expresses by saying that Melchisedech was "without father, without mother, without genealogy." The same idea is expressed by the Apostle, when speaking of Christ, the eternal Priest, he shows Him to belong to the tribe of Juda, " of which no one gave attendance at the altar," which translation of Priesthood brought about therefore a translation of the law.

Third: The third essential feature of the same order is that the Pontiff's oblation is that of bread and wine. This essential characteristic of the everlasting order of Priesthood, although not so interesting to the Jewish priests or nation as the foregoing, is the most striking for us. In Abraham's day God raised up a Priest to offer bread and wine, a typical oblation on the same spot where Christ instituted the Eucharistic sacrifice. The blood of animals slain on the Levitical altar foreshadowed the coming Sacrifice of the Son of God, but the oblation of bread and wine by Melchisedech was typical of the unseen presence of the Divine Victim on the Christian altar.

Fourth: Having outlined these distinguishing features of the order of Melchisedech, I now come to the one with which I am most concerned in this discourse, namely, that the Pontiff of the order of Melchisedech, besides being Priest is also King.

St. Paul quotes from Genesis: "For this Melchisedech was King of Salem, priest of the most High God . . . who first by interpretation of his name is King of Justice, and then also King of Salem, that is King of Peace." This then is also an essential feature of the order of Melchisedech which distinguishes from the order of Aaron. For in the former the priestly and Kingly dignities are combined in the one person, whereas in the latter the Law makes no provision for the sceptre on behalf of the priesthood, but according to the national prophecy of Jacob it is to be held principally by another tribe, that of Juda, and in fact was held as an hereditary right, by the successors of David, the first King of the said tribe. It may possibly be objected, but was Melchisedech any more than a nominal King? Had he a kingdom or real territorial independence? If anyone were bold enough to make such an objection, it would suffice to answer, that history has nowhere put on record the existence of a king of no place, or of an honorary king or of a king in partibus; that such an empty title would not be mentioned in Scripture nor repeated by the Apostle when insisting on the character of the priest, whose order was typical of, or rather identical with, Christ's. That Melchisedech without his kingship would be unrecognisable, and that his kingship is as essential as his Priesthood in order to his being recognised. But there is a plainer answer. Melchisedech was King of Salem just as truly as Bara was King of Sodom or Bersa King of Gomorrha. And Salem is the ancient name of the city of Jerusalem. Melchisedech then was truly King and in the enjoyment of a real territory and capital, whose name explains why its Pontiff-King took no part in the wars of the other Kings, but considered it his part to bless the righteous and victorious Abraham. All possible doubt as to the Kingly character of Melchisedech being removed, it remains clear that an essential feature of his order, which is the order of Christ, is the combination of the Pontifical and Kingly characters and dignities. And this feature is nowhere found in the Levitical order. The Priests for a time combined the office of Prince or Chief Ruler with the sacerdotal office, but besides the fact that such authority was delegated from the Jews, never was a High Priest saluted or recognised as King. Having passed in review the essential features of the eternal Priesthood of Melchisedech and dwelt particularly on his combined dignity as Pontiff-King, we may now, dear brethren, turn with love and reverence to Christ and to His Vicar and view these essential features in the head of the everlasting Priesthood.

CHRIST IS PONTIFF-KING.

We have it from David's inspired pen : "Thou art a Priest for ever according to the order of Melchisedech." But some timid inquirer might suggest the question : Did Christ really possess all the essential features or characteristic powers of the order of Melchisedech ? To which common sense at once replies : Certainly. For a portion of the features or characteristic powers of an order are not that order, which must be taken in its integrity or forfeit all reality. Remove from the order of Melchise dech its Kingly character and it becomes unrecognisable and drops out of existence. Since Christ then belongs to the order of Melchisedech, and Melchisedech is Pontiff-King, so is Christ Pontiff-King. It is impossible that the other characteristics of the order should apply to Christ, this remarkable one alone excepted.

PETER, AFTER ASSOCIATION WITH CHRIST, WAS PONTIFF-KING.

The above reasoning applies also to the Vicar of Christ. If the order of Christ be that of Melchisedech, then is the order of the New Testament identical with it. The order of Christ has its succession of Pontiffs like the order of Aaron. To these Christ transmits His Priesthood, not through genealogical succession, but individually, and with all its characteristic powers. If Christ transmitted the Priesthood without the Kingly character, He would not transmit the Priesthood of Melchisedech. The order of Melchisedech, destined to be everlasting, is that of the Catholic Church. The plenitude of characteristic powers must reside in the Pontiff, for the Pontiff's character determines that of the whole body and Hierarchy. Christ then could not confer, or rather transfer, the plenitude of spiritual power to Peter, His first Vicar, without endowing him also with the Kingly character and dignity, which carries with it territorial independence. Therefore the order of Christ, which is that of Melchisedech, to which the Roman Pontiffs belong, constitutes them Kings and therefore gives them a territorial independence.

If this be revealed truth we should be able to trace the Kingly dignity of Christ and of His Vicar and ascertain how they came by it. And there is plenty of evidence at hand for the purpose. We shall trace elsewhere Christ's Kingly dignity as a necessity in the order of society created by God. We shall trace it in prophecy. We shall gather it from contemporary witnesses, and from the lips of the Saviour Himself. But before examining this most consoling evidence in the times we live in, we may, as a preliminary question connected with the order of Melchisedech, trace the Kingly character of the Redeemer in what I believe to be the reason of one of the great contrasts between the two orders and the two laws, namely, the divided authority of the old law and the united authority of the new.

For this reason or mystical meaning I go to St. Paul. He declares that "all these things happened to them in figure." If all, therefore probably this divided authority under a single legislation.

Christ's Kingly Dignity Traced to Reason of Divided Authority of Old Law and United Authority of New.

And what was such divided authority moulding the one people under the same Divine legislation a figure of? It seems to me it was a figure of what was wanted and to come; the union of the two elements of the sacred humanity together and to the second Divine Person and of their respective functions for the redemption of mankind. " Drop down dew, ye Heavens, from above, and let the clouds rain the just ; (His holy soul) let the earth be opened, and bud forth a Saviour (His sacred body)."

Look back then, dear brethren, sixteen centuries before the coming of Christ to the early days of our race and behold God, ever the Saviour of men, preparing the Redemption to come. Out of the twelve tribes, the offspring of Jacob, two, I cannot find better words, are preeminently pre-destined. Listen to the prophetical blessing bestowed respectively upon Juda and upon Levi. "Thou hast couched as a lion and lioness, who shall rouse him ?" says the Patriarch blessing his son Juda, "the sceptre shall not be taken away from Juda nor a ruler from his thigh, till He come that is to be sent, and He shall be the expectation of nations."

Here is a blessing all temporal, physical and political, winding up with a prophecy of the sleep and the resurrection of the body of the Redeemer taken from the tribe of Juda. He alone slept as a lion in His death, and none could rouse Him but His own Divine Person.

But of Levi the Patriarch says : " I will divide them in Jacob and scatter them in Israel." There is no temporal blessing, but rather a temporal curse for Levi's posterity. The Levites are to inherit no tribal portion of the promised land, but then God draws good out of evil and through Jacob bestows a spiritual blessing in compensation for the temporal punishment or deprivation. For the Levitical tribe will be the soul of their brethren in Israel, scattered indeed throughout the whole national body. And when the limbs are broken away and the heart and head alone remain in the enduring tribe of Juda, that Levitical soul will cling to what remains and with Juda will live on in mutual preservation. The two tribes receive opposite blessings, the one to carry and represent the earthly or temporal life of the coming Saviour, the other to energize with His spiritual life. The former to transmit the blood, to hand down the sceptre, to defend His temporal interests, to fix His country and birthplace and determine His earthly rights and social position. The latter to anticipate the work of His soul, to forego earthly rights, to bow before His Heavenly Father, to offer up His blood for the various wants of mankind in typical sacrifices. Such anticipation and separation of His temporal and spiritual life and of their respective functions in the national life of the people of God was not the work of man. It was the love of the second Divine Person preluding the work of Redemption that did it. And as long as He had not assumed a united body and soul in the mystery of the Incarnation, so long did the temporal and spiritual elements remain separate in the life and government of His people. But when the sacred humanity of the Son of God appeared and Christ had reached the plenitude of His age, it was fitting also that the theocracy should cease to contain two separate elements of government and distinct sources of authority under the single Divine legislation. And if such be the reason of a divided authority under the old law, then do we understand why Christ holds both the sceptre and the priesthood in the perfection of the new. "For the priesthood being translated, it is necessary that a translation also be made of the Law."

II.—That the Roman Pontiffs were actually associated in the person of Peter in the supreme independence of the Son of Man, and therefore in His earthly freedom.

CHRIST'S KINGSHIP A SOCIAL NECESSITY.

God alone, my dear brethren, is supremely independent. Independence, in other words, is a Divine attribute. It means exemption from control, power, direction, influence, or support. Christ being God enjoys this supreme independence. But Christ led also a human life. He was truly man. He had a country with a definite lawful position therein like other men. For this is essential to man. God, who hath created society, is likewise the author of the lawful position of citizens and of the lawful position of rulers. And there is none other created by God. Christ therefore in His own country could only be lawful subject or lawful Prince. Let us suppose for one moment that He was lawful subject. If so, He was bound to the Levitical Priesthood as well as to the political power, bound to pay tribute to the temple and bound to pay tribute to Cæsar, bound therefore to contribute to the preservation of the Old Law and forbidden to procure its abolition. It will be seen at once that there is utter incompatibility between His subjection as man and His independence as God. In other words, it is inconceivable that the Son of Man on account of His Sovereign Divine Power and independence among His fellow-men should not be possessed likewise of Sovereign earthly power and independence and therefore of the lawful position of King. For the former could not be exercised or vindicated by the God-Man without the latter.

DIVINE VINDICATION OF THE KINGLY RIGHT OF CHRIST AND HIS CHIEF APOSTLE.

We are now about to consider how Christ vindicated for Himself and for His Chief Apostle this right to supreme earthly freedom. But we must bear in mind that as Our Lord transmitted the identical Divine truth under various parables because of its various aspects, so did He transfer or intimate the transference of His supreme power to His Vicar under various comparisons or images because of its various relations.

Thus the Chief Apostle received communication of the spiritual firmness symbolized by the rock as a foundation for the spiritual structure of the Church. He received the spiritual care of the whole flock in the command to feed both sheep and lambs. He received the universal spiritual power of binding and loosing with the metaphorical keys. And as a remedy against Satanic sifting of the Church, he received the power and was imposed the duty of confirming the whole Hierarchy in the Faith resulting from the prayer for the infallibility of himself in particular and his successors. On all these occasions the Chief Apostle received communication of the Supreme Power that was in Christ. But Supreme Power besides these positive relations has negative ones. Supreme Power is also supreme independence. In God it is inherent and absolute. In man, who is finite, it must be delegated and relative. In Christ there was inherent and absolute independence, which called for a corresponding supreme earthly freedom. The supreme spiritual power transmitted to the Chief Apostle has also its counterpart in supreme earthly independence. Independence of spiritual control and influence, independence of temporal control and influence. I will then introduce you, dear brethren, to a most wonderful and pleasing scene wherein you will discover the supreme rights of the Son of Man and the association of Peter in the same rights. It is only another of those occasions wherein the Chief Apostle's supremacy is declared and vindicated.

We read in St. Matthew, chapter xvii. : " And when they were come to Capharnaum, they that received the didrachmas came to Peter, and said to him : Doth not your master pay the didrachma ? He said : Yes. And when he was come into the house, Jesus prevented him saying : What is thy opinion, Simon ? Of whom do the Kings of the earth take tribute or custom ? Of their own children, or of strangers ? And he said : Of strangers. Jesus said to him : Then the children are free. But that we may not scandalize them, go thou to the sea, and cast in a hook ; and that fish which shall first come up, take ; and when thou hast opened its mouth thou shalt find a stater ; take that, and give it to them for Me and thee."

In this scene on the shore of the lake depicted by the inspired pen you behold the most admirable manifestation of the Divine Power of Christ, yet with a definite ulterior object. For why, may we ask reverently, was the Divine Power exerted on this occasion ? Was it principally in self-manifestation or not rather to shield the human rights of the Son of Man ? For on the same occasion you have recorded the declaration of the supreme earthly right of Jesus Christ and of His Vicar : " Then the children are free." Christ instructed His Chief Apostle as to the supremacy of His freedom before vindicating it. Before Peter had time to report to his Divine Master the reply he unwarily gave to the tax-gatherers or to carry Him their request, Christ anticipated His Chief Apostle on the very subject and elicited from him the opinion that the children of the Kings of the earth are free from the payment of tribute or custom. Here then is a comparison instituted between the Kings of the earth and their children on the one hand and the Lord of the temple, for which the tax was gathered, and Jesus Christ and His Chief Apostle on the other. If the Kings of the earth do not take tribute or custom from their own children, neither does the Lord God from His Divine Son made man nor from the Apostle associated in His freedom. Here it will be useful to

bear in mind what has been said of the necessarily
definite and lawful position of Christ as man within
His own country. The Jews who believed Christ to
be God, believed in His supreme right, for who will
deny or misconstrue the supreme Divine right? But
the earthly right of Christ as man was liable to be
misunderstood and in fact was on this occasion being
invaded. Rather than this should be the Son of God
resolved to pay as God :* " Volle pagare da Dio." The
first fish that comes to the hook is the treasurer of the
Son of God for this occasion. The human purse
carried by Judas is dispensed with, not because Judas
will betray his Divine Master, but because Christ
on this occasion hath resolved not to pay as man.
Now I reason thus : If Christ were subject as
man at this period of His life, His Divine freedom
would not exempt Him from the duty of a subject.
Christ did not so teach, who deemed it became Him " to
fulfil all justice," whom " it behoved in all things to be
made like His brethren," who was " one tempted in all
things like as we are, yet without sin," who before His
public ministry, that is, before He came into the exercise
of His supreme rights, was subject to His parents, who,
even on the threshold of His public ministry, acknowledged the authority over Him of John the Baptist.
Christ nevertheless had recourse to a miracle on this
great occasion to avoid yielding the obedience of an
earthly subject. If so, and who can deny it, what lesson
could more significantly set forth the sovereign earthly
right of the Son of Man? The Lord who loved to waive
every right, to take the place of a servant at the feet of
His Apostles, to appear not only as a subject, but as an
outcast, was also the Divine teacher of man and the
Founder of the New Law and the Introducer of the new
Priestly order. Hence the reason for declaring and
vindicating His earthly supremacy and that of His Chief
Apostle.

* Mastai Ferretti. Gli evangelisti uniti.

Association of Peter in Christ's Kingly Right.

We have seen, dear brethren, from what has been said : First—That the exercise of Divine independence and Power in Christ is inconceivable without corresponding earthly freedom and supremacy; and Second—That Christ on a celebrated occasion vindicated not His right as God, since He paid as God, but His supreme earthly right as man and Son of the Lord of the temple.

As St. Peter is associated in the declaration and vindication of the earthly right of the Son of the Lord of the temple, let us now look more closely into that association.

If you remember the words of the text from St. Matthew, it will occur to you, dear brethren, that Peter is not merely the instrument of Christ for the performance of the miracle, but that he is a sharer, first, in the material object of it, second, in the benefit of it, and third, in the purpose of it.

First : He is a sharer in the material object of the miracle. The Chief Apostle, and he alone, is called upon to give for himself what he gives for Christ. "Give it to them for Me and thee." The stater or silver tetradrachm being equal to twice the didrachma and therefore to twice the tax for one person, Peter obtained as well as his Divine Master the wherewith to apparently pay the tax. The amount is not levied on his earnings, he loses nothing by paying the tribute, subtracts nothing from his means, whatever they were or might have been. Which amounts to saying, that neither Peter nor his Divine Master have been taxed. Those who receive the didrachma, receive from Peter a silver coin equal to the taxation of two persons, but neither from Peter nor from Christ do they get it as a tribute, for neither have really been taxed. Peter therefore is here associated with Christ in his remaining untaxed according to the meaning and intent of the law and therefore in His earthly freedom.

Second: Peter is a sharer in the benefit of the miracle: the avoiding of scandal. "That we may not scandalize them, go thou to the sea. . ." Those who received the tribute, as well as those who employed them, were quite unprepared to admit Christ's right of exemption or that of His Chief Apostle. They were no doubt also unfit as yet to be enlightened on the subject. There was nothing therefore to do but to yield to their demand or to present the appearance of doing so, if the appearance of insubordination were to be avoided. Peter is associated with his Divine Master in avoiding the appearance of insubordination, by presenting the appearance of earthly subjection. Now, a good subject should not only wish to avoid the scandal of refusing to pay tribute, but he should be also willing to pay what he is bound. But Peter is associated with Christ in a proceeding which reveals no anxiety to pay the tribute, but only to avoid the scandal. Therefore Peter is associated with Christ in his exemption from tribute. Therefore the Chief Apostle is no longer subject to the temple or Jewish Priesthood or Levitical law, but he is raised from subjection to the old order to partnership in the new.

Third: Peter is associated with Christ in the purpose for which the miracle was wrought, namely the safe guarding of the supreme spiritual and temporal earthly freedom of those who are compared to, although they rank higher than, the children of the Kings of the earth. The vindicating of this freedom for His Apostle was so important in the Divine plan, that it must be secured, cost what it might. There would be scandal! Then let scandal be removed by a Divine payment. It only cost Christ a few words and some prayer to bestow upon His Chief Apostle the plenitude of spiritual power and the perfection of Doctrinal Infallibility in the church, but to vindicate his supreme independence it cost nothing less than a miracle. But I foresee a possible objection. I may be told: your reasoning proves no doubt the spiritual independence and supremacy of the Vicar of

Christ, and so far his earthly freedom, but you have yet to show that his temporal or political freedom was declared or vindicated on the occasion.

To which I reply that Peter was associated in the same freedom which Christ, his Master, vindicated for Himself. But Christ could not vindicate spiritual supremacy and exemption, without at the same time vindicating temporal supremacy and exemption. For according to St. Paul : " The priesthood being translated, it is necessary that a translation also be made of the Law." Claiming independence of one therefore was claiming independence of the other. And for the same reason the tribute to be paid to the temple, although purely spiritual so far as it was paid for the Divine worship and spiritual rule, was temporal and political insomuch as it was enforced by the co-ordinate authorities of the Priesthood and the sceptre under the one national legislation of Israel. Therefore refusing as man to pay the tribute to the temple and associating Peter in the same right is tantamount to vindicating for the Chief Apostle both spiritual and political independence. But supreme spiritual independence constitutes Peter Supreme Pontiff, and supreme political independence constitutes him King. Therefore like his Divine Master he is Pontiff-King.

Possibly my supposed objector might still feel inclined to insist, saying : No doubt Christ as man could not have been a subject in His Country, but must have held both spiritual and temporal supreme power, since He translated both the Priesthood and the Law, but what proves that He on the occasion associated Peter in both supreme powers? Well, two reasons: First—Because He declared and vindicated His supreme freedom as man in respect to both spiritual and political authorities on the same important occasion, and simultaneously associated His Chief Apostle in the declaration and vindication of the identical freedom. " Then the children are free," and " give it to them for Me and for thee." Second—Because if Peter and his successors were not associated both in spiritual and temporal independence, then there would not be translation both of the Priesthood and of the Law, but only of the Priesthood to the New Testament. Then the plenitude of authority inherited by Christ from the Old Law would not have passed to the New. Christ, to whom as man is given all power in Heaven and on earth, inherited all the spiritual and temporal authority with which God had invested the leaders of His people. Such authority was divided by the Mosaic legislation between the heir to the sceptre and the heir to the priestly rule. Christ abolished the co-ordinate authorities with their imperfections and their shadows by gathering God's one authority over body and soul, over time and eternity, to Himself. He combined, or more truly united, in Himself the authority of the Jewish sceptre and the authority of the Levitical priesthood, and translated the united authority under the order of Melchisedech to the future rulers of His Church in the person of His Chief Apostle. Therefore the Roman Pontiffs were actually associated in the person of Peter in the supreme independence of the Son of Man, and therefore in His earthly and temporal freedom.

HOW FACTS CORRESPOND WITH RIGHTS.

In the first argument it was proved that the order of Christ which is that of Melchisedech, to which the Roman Pontiffs belong, constitutes them Kings and therefore gives them a territorial independence. In both arguments, which rest on different texts of Scripture and are quite independent, a distinct principle is conveyed, namely : the Kingly right of Christ and of the Supreme Pontiff of the New Law. But rights so far as they are acknowledged become embodied in facts. The facts therefore should square with the Kingly right both of Christ and His Vicar. The History of the Catholic Church will supply the great, luminous, constant, central fact, which is the embodiment of the Kingly right of Christ's Vicar on earth, namely : the civil or temporal Princedom and Patrimony of St. Peter, also called the temporal Power of the Pope.

" Thou Art the King of Israel."

I will now, dear brethren, proceed to consider how far the Kingly right of Jesus Christ is acknowledged and becomes a fact of history, how it is hailed by friends, or disavowed, charged against Him, and derided by enemies. Needless to inquire how witnesses friendly or hostile come to the knowledge of the Kingly right of Jesus Christ. Whether through acquiring the knowledge of His Divinity they naturally infer his supreme human right, or whether they learn it from prophecy, or pick it up from the tradition of their race or from Christ's own testimony.

No sooner had Nathanael believed His Divine Nature than he saluted Him also as King : " Rabbi, thou art the Son of God, thou art the King of Israel." Again, as he approached Jerusalem after raising Lazarus, the multitude came forth to meet Him, saluting Him and saying : " Blessed be the King, who cometh in the name of the Lord," and " Blessed be the Kingdom of our father David that cometh." And the prophet, who in the distance of time saw His poverty as He rode into Jerusalem, failed not to mention His rank : " Fear not, daughter of Sion ; behold thy King cometh sitting on an ass's colt."

Jesus of Nazareth the King of the Jews.

I shall possibly be met by the objection founded on the words of the Divine Prisoner : " My Kingdom is not of this world." But on careful inspection it will be found that these words of the Divine Prisoner in the Hall of Pilate harmonize completely with the claims of the Divine Teacher and Vindicator of right at Capharnaum, and with the essential characteristics of the everlasting order of Priesthood.

Let us approach the subject with loving reverence, dear brethren, lifting the eyes of Faith upon the Divine Captive, imploring Him to cast upon us, as upon the Apostle, one look, which may make us hate sin for ever. The Governor has been called outside to the Jews, who would not enter the Hall. In answer to his inquiry the Jews say : "If He were not a malefactor, we would not have delivered Him up to thee." On returning to the Hall, Pilate, according to St. John, simply inquires : "Art thou the King of the Jews?" And Jesus, putting the Governor to the test, by giving him a chance of stating his own opinion, says : "Sayest thou this of thyself, or have others told it thee of Me?" "Am I a Jew?" is the scornful reply of the representative of the usurping power and the indignant outburst of a guilty conscience in self-defence, which told that Christ's question was a thrust home. And now again : "Thy own nation and the chief priests have delivered thee up to me, what hast thou done?" Jesus answered : "My Kingdom is not of this world. If My Kingdom were of this world, My servants would certainly strive that I should not be delivered to the Jews : but now My Kingdom is not hence." Pilate therefore said to Him : "Art thou King then?" Jesus answered : "Thou sayest that I am King. For this was I born, and for this came I into the world, that I should give testimony unto the truth." Let us now examine this confession of the Divine Prisoner. Before clearly stating that He is King, although He has implied as much, by referring the case to Pilate's conscience, Christ declares : "My Kingdom is not of this world." Observe, He says not : "My Kingdom is not in this world," but, "of this world." An indirect reply to the previous question concerning His Kingship and a direct one to the statement of Pilate that His nation had delivered Him up. "My Kingdom is not of this world," which obviously means : "My Kingly right is not of this world." I waive My right and choose not to enforce it by appeal to My servants and to violence, as is the custom of the Princes of this world. My people will not have Me to reign over them. The suffrage of the nation is not in My favour. My right is built up neither on the force nor on the suffrage of this world. Mine is a Heavenly Sanctioned right. My earthly Kingship is subordinate to My Divine rule, therefore I would reign over a willing people; "but now My Kingdom is not hence." Pilate therefore said to Him: "Art thou a King then?" And here comes the straight reply of Christ: "Thou sayest that I am King." As a lover of subjection, Our Lord would again have preferred to conceal His right, but as "having been born and having come into this world that He should give testimony unto the truth," He could not withhold it from the conditionally sanctioned authority claiming to hear it. Pilate need not have inquired again: "What is the truth?" Had he been willing he might have discovered it in every word uttered before his Court by the King of the Jews.

But the whole history of the Passion, dear brethren, gives loud testimony of the Kingly character of the Saviour of mankind. Had Christ, as man, and inhabitant of the land given to Abraham, His father, been a subject only among His fellow citizens, if the thing were conceivable, had He clearly disclaimed all earthly title, so that no Jew might suspect Him of possessing any power or freedom below the God-Head with His Father, what charge, I ask you, could the Jews have brought against Him to interest the Political and usurping Power, and to screen, if it had been possible, their Heaven-opposing malice stirred to its depths by a higher claim, for which alone they had twice condemned Him in the Council of the Nation? What would have been the meaning or import of the mock King, saluted, sceptred, and crowned? The Jews were Regicides as well as Deicides, although Regicides because Deicides.

The Saviour was both adored and persecuted at His birth as being the King of the Jews by men who knew Him by no other title, and the title was written over the instrument of His torture. Vain were the efforts of the Chief Priests to destroy its significance. Not: "He said, I am King of the Jews," but "Jesus of Nazareth, the King of the Jews," remained written in the languages of the world.

The unfortunate Governor's sin was that of weakness. No one to my knowledge has been more severe with him. Who reads the Passion goes cordially with him in his persistent efforts to declare the innocence of the Just man. His attitude and his words to the Jews give striking proof that they had not, in the accusations they brought against Him, put their real grievance in the foreground. The Governor was not impressed with the charge of active rivalship with Cæsar, nor with the accusing nation's loyalty to his Imperial Master. And he seemed to make it his business to punish the Deicides for their duplicity. "Behold your King," said he, and again as they insisted: "Shall I crucify your King?" And when the deed was being done, when no doubt Pilate still better realized his sin, he further punished the nation by annulling, as far as in him lay, his own act, and the political charge brought against the Saviour. The inscription written by himself in the three languages was no indictment, but an opposite declaration. And he stood by it: "What I have written, I have written."

CHRIST THE LAST BEARER OF THE SCEPTRE OF JUDA.

But such Kingly right should not only be borne out by the facts of acknowledgment. It should agree also with all the conditions of civil and national local right. Let us examine how Christ could civilly and politically come by this earthly power and freedom. We have seen that God is the author of society and therefore of all legitimate rights whether bestowed by or inherited in the nation. He is only the Permitter of usurpation. The Kingly right of Christ was not a usurped right, nor was it bestowed by the nation, which rejected Him, therefore it must have been an inherited right. It must have been the right of the Jewish rulers and of the Jewish nation. And such inherited right of the Son of David and of the Son of Juda was clearly attested by the National prophecy. "The sceptre shall not be taken away from Juda nor a ruler from his thigh till He come." This does not mean that the sceptre should depart before Christ could inherit it, nor that violence or subjugation could snatch away a God-given right. The great national prophecy evidently alludes to the termination of the old order of things, when both the Law and the priesthood should be translated. The sceptre then was safely carried down to Christ. The tribe of Juda had alone endured for that purpose, returning after the Captivity with a small remnant of Benjamin and Levi, the latter to be at its service for the ministry of the temple. Not only the ancestral line of Christ, the guarding of which was the main purpose of the national organization, but the ruling power of the organized tribe, endured, whoever may have been in right the holders of the sceptre, and remained vested in the leading Jewish families. True, the power of the priests seemed paramount within the nation after the Captivity, but, as already abundantly shown, the Priestly authority was at most only co-ordinate with the power of the sceptre, for " which is greater, he that sitteth at table, or he that serveth ? Is not he that sitteth at table ? And again it should not be forgotten when comparing the relative importance of the two tribes of Juda and Levi, that the former did really hand down with the sceptre the elements of which the sacred body of the Redeemer was formed, whereas the latter which foreshadowed the spiritual functions of His Holy soul had nothing to hand down but a shadow. Thus not before Christ transferred elsewhere both the Priesthood and the Sovereign rule was the sceptre taken away from Juda. What though His sceptre were a reed or His crown one of thorns ? His enemies, by seeking to destroy His title, only published it to the world. Jesus the Son of David was therefore the last bearer of the sceptre of Juda.

TRANSLATION OF THE LAW AND THE PRIESTHOOD.

We have seen, dear brethren, that the Kingly right of Christ did not remain a mere principle, that it was borne out by the facts of the acknowledgment of friends and could not be smothered by the hatred, disavowal, or derision of enemies. We then proceeded to examine how Christ's claim to Kingly rank harmonized with local right. We have now to consider how the translation of right from the old Law to the New is embodied in the facts of history. Let us go back for a moment to the National prophecy. The Holy Patriarch's words are : " The sceptre shall not be taken away." You will observe that the word "taken away " or " depart " from Juda, does not mean " die out " or " be destroyed " or " cease altogether "; the idea conveyed by these expressions is one of transference, not of destruction or cessation. And the prophetical blessing agrees with the historical statement of one equally inspired. What Jacob expresses by the words "taken away," St. Paul expresses by the word "translation." The two expressions, I take it, were moulded by two aspects of the identical truth. Jesus Christ of the tribe of Juda, "of which no one gave attendance at the altar," without renouncing or forfeiting the power symbolized by the sceptre, gathered to Himself the spiritual power of the priesthood by becoming Himself Pontiff, and transmitted to Peter His undivided Sacerdotal and Kingly Power. " For the priesthood being translated, it is necessary that a translation also be made of the Law."

But there is not only translation of power to men of a New order, there is also translation of the New order to a New territory. St. Peter goes to Rome. Here is an historical fact which embodies more than the mere translation of the Law and the Priesthood. We shall see that St. Peter went forth with no empty title, but with a territorial right. For the Priestly and Kingly authority is transferred from Juda and Jerusalem to the centre of the Gentile world. The works of God are complete and break not down in the middle.*

God said to Abraham : " To thy seed will I give this land;" the Roman power subjugated that land, violated the right of the sceptre, and sentenced to death the King

---

* " Do not think that I am come to destroy the law or the Prophets. I am not come to destroy, but to fulfil."

of the Jews. What more could they have done to forfeit sovereignty at the head of the empire? The eloquence of facts is too great to leave any doubt about the existence of right. We think of God's ways and exclaim: a fair and providential exchange! Who enlightened the Roman sage, or what tradition did he come across to know that some would come from Judea, who should succeed to the mastery at the head-quarters of Imperial Power?

Thus after being associated with Christ, Peter comes under the New order, which as Divinely sworn shall last for ever. The fisherman moves forth from Salem to take possession of the great empire-city, which his order will transform into a city of Peace. As priest of the Most High God, he will there offer the bread and wine of the sacrifice of the New Testament. You may not trace his right or dignity to his race as the Jewish Pontiff's of old. For he is "without father or mother or genealogy" in his succession to the Pontificate and his successors after him." "The Lord hath sworn and He will not repent. Thou art, a Priest for ever according to the order of Melchisedech." He carries with him from Sion the Priesthood, the Law, and sceptre, and settles them at the head-quarters of the enemies of the Jewish nation. "The Lord will send forth the sceptre of thy power out of Sion : rule thou in the midst of thy enemies."

If hypothesis were not out of place it might be interesting to consider how events would have shaped if the Jewish nation had not been scattered. Theologians have gone so far as to suppose Christ redeeming the world without passing through Death. I will suppose that a Jewish faction had alone been guilty of Deicide, that no punishment had fallen on the nation as such, that the Jews had remained in their land, that no foreign power had usurped local rights. What would have been the consequence? The Law and the Priesthood would have passed out of the former hands to the successors of the Prince of the Apostles; so far we are certain. But then no reason appears for the dereliction of the land given to the people of God from the beginning. The Chief Apostle's See must have been the throne of David. The whole Jewish Constitution would have been merged into the paternal Government of the Pontiff-King. The Pontificate would have been open to any tribe. The Patrimony of St. Peter would have been the Holy Land. Christians would have been called after Salem and not after Rome. The hypothesis indeed seems necessary to explain the expectations of the nation and the promises which gave rise to them.

The people evidently believed before and after Christ's resurrection that the Theocracy was not abandoned, that God would sooner or later vindicate His right to the Government of one state for the good of the world. We have gathered as much from the shouts of the multitude hailing their King : " Blessed be the Kingdom of our Father David that cometh." A temporal Government under the immediate control of Christ was the natural and legitimate expectation of the early Church instructed in all things spiritual and preparing for the baptism of the Holy Ghost : " Lord," said the assembled Apostles, " wilt Thou at this time restore again the Kingdom to Israel ? " Christ denied not that the restoration would take place, but He indicated neither the time nor the manner.

Although the Pontificate of the New order is not inherited by tribal right, but is open to all nations, the fact of the Jewish race constituting the mother Church would have brought many sons of David through spiritual right to the succession of the everlasting throne of their Father. It depended only on their fidelity. Such expectations were not incompatible with the instructions Christ had given. In the following words of the 131st Psalm we have, with the absolute promise that Christ the Son of David should succeed to his throne, a conditional promise concerning his children and concerning Sion for all time. " The Lord hath sworn truth to David, and He will not make it void ; of the fruit of thy womb I will set upon thy throne. If thy children will keep My covenant, and these My testimonies, which I shall teach them ; their children also for evermore shall sit upon thy throne. For the Lord hath chosen Sion : He hath chosen it for His dwelling. This is My rest for ever and ever : here will I dwell, for I have chosen it."

But the children of David did not keep the covenant. Christ's brethren sold Him and resolved His death. The Jews forfeited their right to constitute the mother and mistress Christian Church. The Gentiles were allowed to scatter the nation and raze the Holy City, but in return were called upon to yield Rome and its Sovereignty for the Pontiff-King of the Christian Church. Salem was and Rome is the Holy City. We are not children of Peace, but of the Sword.

LIMITATION OF TERRITORIAL RIGHT.

But here some critic might put me to the test by the following objection : You have spoken of the temporal freedom in Christ and in His Vicar as a result of the supreme earthly independence of the Son of Man. What have you to say of the positive relations of the same earthly supremacy? In other words, does not Christ as man inherit the plenitude of temporal power on earth? To this I reply that Christ only laid claim to temporal rule in the country which belonged to Him by ancestral right, and which became through foreign usurpation the foundation of the temporal patrimony of His Vicar in the land of the usurper. No doubt to Christ is given all power in Heaven and on earth. But having given to earthly Kings their temporal rights, He does not withdraw as man what He has given as God. His territorial right was therefore limited, and so is that of His Vicar.

As for the universal arbitration of the Pontiff, which is quite a distinct question, there have been signs that such an event is possible, and nothing more desirable can be conceived for the peace of mankind.

THE PAPACY, THE WORLD, AND THE REVOLUTION.

The Papacy as it presents itself to the world is the greatest human fact. The genius of man unassisted by Faith, in presence of this fact, has dictated lines which rise almost to the beauty of Biblical poetry and prophetic language. Statesmen of various creeds, familiar with the Government of nations, have surveyed the fact without reference to right and have said: that is well done, that is a necessity; a universal Church spread among the nations cannot be subject to any one of them, therefore its Chief authority must be free.

We also, dear brethren, conclude to the necessity of the Pope's freedom from his universal rule, but we rest that spiritual rule on a Divine institution. I have introduced this argument when treating of Christ's Kingship as a social necessity. It is the familiar theme of eloquent preachers and able Catholic writers. My business has been to endeavour to show you that besides this inferential proof of the necessity of the Pope's temporal power there is contained in Holy Scripture a positive declaration and a Divine vindication of the Pontiff's Kingly character and Princely freedom.

You will conclude then that the constant and luminous central fact of Church history, the temporal Sovereignty enjoyed by the successors of Peter, is not merely the outcome of the good will of Christian nations, nor a provisional state to be succeeded by some more enlightened agreement with rulers of the nineteenth century, but that it is indeed the use, exercise, and actuation of a Divinely bestowed right and power, which Christ also vindicates from age to age.

Christ waived His own rights as King so far as was compatible with His office of Divine teacher and Founder of the Church, but it was to secure the peaceable exercise of the same rights in His representative on earth. He would not have miraculously vindicated and upheld the Princely right of His Vicar unless He had intended such right to be exercised for the freedom of His church in the midst of a strife-loving world.

I alluded in the beginning of this lecture to the present state of the Pontiff. He is in the hands of the worst enemy that has appeared since the world was ruled by the heathen. It is the spirit of national apostasy or the revolution. Men have cast off the yoke of religion and personal authority from their new society. They are driven by the fever of a godless nationalism, wherein they imagine to secure worldly greatness. The evil reaches its climax in the secret hatred of revealed Religion, and of the Pontiff its Chief exponent and Divine foundation. This hatred is embodied and energizing in dark societies, which drive men unconsciously against the Church and against the Pontiff. It is the rebellion of men who hate God, and would prefer any rule rather than His. It is a repetition of history. "We have no King but Cæsar," says the revolted nation. We will own no authority but that which is secular, we will salute no symbol but that of independence.

And thus the Italian revolution, like the Apostasy elsewhere, has been steadily doing the work of the evil one. Short of personal violence to the Pope, which would not be safe for the nation, the revolution has undone the work of God, the civil Princedom, respected in all Christian ages.

Not a remnant is left to Leo of the patrimony of St. Peter. He enjoys the independence of his palace as any important subject might in a civilized country. But, if I mistake not, his Sovereignty is in nowise acknowledged, but in every way violated and insulted. Violated and insulted by foreign swords at his very gates, violated and insulted by the intrusion of foreign courts of justice, violated and insulted by a foreign coin and a foreign stamp, violated and insulted by the perilous prospect of being shut out from communication with the rest of the world should the usurper engage in hostilities with other earthly powers : in one word, violated and insulted by the sacrilegious occupation of a deluded Prince. Your duty is prayer. The duty of constitutional agitation is going on elsewhere. But we may rest assured as regards the event.

The sceptre of Juda was led into Captivity of old, dear brethren, but it returned to its appointed realm. So will the Pontiff's everlasting right be hailed again in the restored Patrimony of St. Peter. Amen.

THE TEMPORAL INHERITANCE OF THE ROMAN CHURCH.

"Semini tuo dabo terram hanc."—GENESIS.

IF there be Scripture evidence relating to the rightful independence of the Holy See, no one will deny that the present day is the opportune time for sifting it. And if the teaching of the Church hitherto on the subject removes it from the domain of ordinary human institutions, nothing is more consistent than to go for information respecting it to that source which records the whole plan of God's dealing with His Church.

With these thoughts I wrote as follows to the *Tablet* on February 22nd, 1890 :—

" I crave your permission to write a few words on the subject of the temporal power of the Pope. After the repeated appeals from the present Pope and his predecessor to the Catholic world on this subject during so many years, it requires no apology to take up the pen to supply, if possible, fresh motives for Catholics to stand together in defence of his temporal rights. The late Encyclical, declaring that 'all are bound to communicate their faith to others, either to the instruction of other Christians, or to their strengthening, or to repel the audacity of those outside the fold,' indicates what kind of warfare on behalf of the Church is expected of the faithful, and that victory will be awarded to faith and to the powerful convictions that spring therefrom. To settle and strengthen our convictions in regard to the sanctity of the Pontiff's rights seems, then, to be of paramount importance if we are 'to repel the audacity of those outside the fold.' But convictions must spring from clearly conceived notions. Can it be said that the inferential proof of the necessity of the temporal power, as a basis of right, is a clearly conceived notion whereon

4

to found solid convictions ? Pius IX. is reported to have said (I have good authority for saying so), 'that it could not be defined that under all circumstances the possession of the temporal power was necessary for the exercise of the spiritual.' If temporal power is not necessary under all circumstances, how is the Pontiff's right to be securely founded upon *the necessity* of the temporal power? Hence vagueness in the minds of many, and want of moral power from want of conviction. Yet we are appealed to, not merely to pray that God may hasten His never-failing protection, but distinctly to bear witness to the Pontiff's temporal rights. They have been claimed as such by Pius IX. and his successor. And the Bishops assembled from all parts of the world and of the United Kingdom in 1862 re-echoed the Pontiff's claim with no uncertain sound :—

"'Vox enim Tua,' they declared, 'quasi tuba Sacerdotalis, toti orbi clangens proclamavit, quod "singulari prorsus divinæ Providentiæ consilio factum sit, ut Romanus Pontifex, quem Christus totius ecclesiæ suæ caput centrumque constituit, civilem assequeretur principatum;" ab omnibus igitur nobis esse pro certissimo tenendum non fortuito hoc regimen temporale Sanctæ Sedi accessisse, sed ex speciali divina dispositione illi esse tributum. . . .'

"The Pontiffs temporal right has a foundation, but that foundation is not the necessity of the temporal power. To put the matter plainly, the Pontiff's temporal power is either the gift of men or the gift of God ; there is no alternative. If the Pontiff's territorial right be the gift of kings or emperors, sanctioned and approved, no doubt —nay more, even brought about—by the kind providence of God for the better spiritual government of the Church, who shall convince Catholics of the intrinsic and inalienable right of the Pontiff to temporal rule? Who shall persuade Catholics that men, who often repent of their gift, may not take back in one century what they have bestowed in another ? We have nothing to do in such case but to pray, as in duty bound, that it may please God to change the hearts of rulers and people, so that, far from interfering with the spiritual government of the Church, they may duly honour it by the surrender of the temporal power over Rome, which alone seems to be its proper guarantee. In such case, no intrinsic or essential right of the Church is violated ; no appeal, therefore, can be made to the Catholic faith and conscience of the universe to vindicate by the power of moral suffrage a right which has never rested on aught but the gift of man. Other princes entrusted with temporal rule have been deprived by the will of the people—why not the Pontiff?

"Very different will be the effect on Catholics if they come to acquire the explicit knowledge that the temporal power is no human institution, governed by a general providence of God, which rules all things for the good of men, but an institution of God's own governed by a peculiar dispensation of Divine Providence. They will feel that the right we contend for rests on a solid basis, that their faith is appealed to, that the usurpation of the States of the Church is truly a sacrilege of the first magnitude. Catholic patriots will discover that their national aspirations must yield to a God-given right. The world itself will give way to the appeal of conscience and of faith, as it has ever done before. For 'this is the victory which overcometh the world, our faith.'

" In a thesis ('The Civil Principality,' by the Rev. C. F. P. Collingridge. Burns and Oates) lately published, it is shown that Christ vindicated for Himself and for the Roman Pontiffs, in the person of Peter, temporal independence and therefore temporal power, and consequently that the temporal power of the Pope is not a human, but a divine institution. With the privilege of the insertion of another letter, I hope to show, in reply to a venerable and not unkind critic, and quite apart from the argument of the thesis, the 'title, translation, and extent of the Pontiff's territorial right.'

"P.S.—The thesis, under the heading 'Divine Vindication of Independence,' takes it for granted that the tribute was payable to the Temple. Those who hold that it was collected for Cæsar or his representative, will see that the same reasoning applies in this case, with this difference, that Christ vindicated His own and His Apostles' independence in respect to a foreign usurper, instead of vindicating it among His own subjects, who failed to recognise His lawful exemption."

In the next issue of the same Catholic paper appeared the following letters. The first, which is, on the whole, favourable, is signed by " Catholic Legitimist." It is as follows :—

" Will you permit me to offer a few words in criticism on Father Collingridge's interesting letter in your issue of February 22nd? Father Collingridge would appear to insist that the Pope's one claim to the temporal power consists in its being the direct gift of God. This most certainly it is, but it should not be forgotten that above and beyond this *immediate* divine sanction, the Pope, considered merely as a temporal sovereign, partakes also of the *mediately* divine sanction conferred by Almighty God on every other legitimate prince or government. We cannot expect Protestants to believe that the temporal power is of directly divine institution ; but we can expect them to believe, with Holy Scripture, that all authority is from above, and that there is thus scriptural warranty for the civil princedom of the Pope equally with, say, the Imperial authority of the reigning family in Austria.

" Father Collingridge would seem to say that if man gave the temporal power, man also could take it away. Does he not for the moment overlook the fact that, as the Church has taught over and over again, *all* authority is of divine sanction? Can any nation, of its own will merely, depose its sovereign ? What says the Syllabus, to go back no further ? Its 63rd Proposition formally condemns the following error : ' *Legitimis Principibus obedientiæ detractare immo et rebellare licet.*' It therefore follows that, even leaving out of the question the directly divine origin of the temporal sovereignty, the Italians had no more right to rebel against the Pope than the French had to expel Charles X.

"Father Collingridge's argument is, of course, the one that will appeal strongly to most Catholics ; but it is well to lose sight of no single fact that can in any way add to the just and obedient claims of the Pope to the States of the Church, and especially when the fact is such as should logically weigh with any Protestant statesman believing in the truth of Holy Scripture."

The second, which contains an unfavourable criticism, is signed " P. K. Q.," and reads thus :—

" Referring to the letter of the Rev. C. F. P. Collingridge, the following quotation from Cardinal Newman's sermon, 'The Pope and the Revolution,' preached on Rosary Sunday, 1866, at Birmingham, may be interesting. ' Now observe . . . no Catholic maintains that the rule of the Pope as a king, in Rome and its provinces, which men are now hoping to take from him, is, strictly speaking, what is called a theocracy, that is, a divine government. This government, indeed, in spiritual matters, in the Catholic Church throughout the world, might be called a theocracy, because he is the Vicar of Christ and has the assistance of the Holy Ghost ; but not such is his kingly rule in his own dominions. . . .' "

Under the heading " Theocracy of the New Law," the following reply appeared in a subsequent number :—

" Sir,—With your permission I will reply to two correspondents, whose criticism I carefully read in your issue of March 1st. The first, signing 'Catholic Legitimist,' criticises a sentence of mine in reference to the temporal power, as though implying that I overlooked the fact that all authority is of divine sanction. The sentence was : 'Who shall persuade Catholics that men, who often repent of their gifts, may not take back in one century what they have bestowed in another ?' Had I added the words : 'without violating a God-given right,' which the context warrants, there would have been no possible room for confusion.

"What I wished to insist upon, and again take occasion now to do, is simply that human governments are so far under human control that they are liable to modifications, subject to the laws which govern civil society. Republics have been transformed into monarchies, and *vice versa ;* whether with the consent of the whole nation, or in violation of some right or rights, is not always distinctly ascertainable. If the Pope's temporal power is subject to such laws, who shall persuade Catholics that what human agency hath established human agency may not disestablish? Without any violation even of human right, a legitimate monarch might, with the consent of the nation, abdicate his throne with a view of transforming the monarchy into a republic, because human monarchy is not above human control. If the Pope is only an ordinary temporal monarch, who shall persuade Catholics that he may not, if he choose, abdicate in like manner? The teaching of the Church, which I would wish to bring more prominently forward, is that the Pope cannot abdicate his temporal right either to human rulers or people, because it is not subject to human laws. Other governments may change hands, or be modified in form, or disappear altogether ; his never. The reason is, to use again the language of the Church, because his civil principality was obtained '*singulari Divinæ Providentiæ consilio,*' and was granted to him '*ex speciali Divina dispositione.*' In other words, his temporal right did not accrue to him from human agency, nor was it acquired by the Pontiff at any time, like the monarchical right of the Christian kingdoms of Europe planted by the Church and consecrated by her unction, but is inherent to his office, which is Christ's own institution.

"Far be it from me, a minister of Christ, to utter a syllable which might detract from the loyalty due to the old Christian monarchies of Europe. Not only does the monarchical form of government best signify to man the monarchy of God, and the term subject most nobly interpret the relation of the creature, but the Christian kingdoms of Europe grew out of the Church and are her legitimate offspring, and therefore the rebellion against this order of things is so far a rebellion against Christ. Even the authority of pagan rulers is sanctioned by God, as we know from the Apostle ; how much more that of Christian monarchs ! But let us not jeopardise the interests of the Papacy by comparing with it even a Christian monarchy. Let us remove all cause of confusion from the minds of Catholics. Those will best consult the interests of Christian monarchy who best consult the interests of the Roman Church, which is the Mother and Mistress of Christian kingdoms and of their respective Churches. I will now take leave of my courteous critic, remarking that what I have supposed him to require, namely, a differentiation between human monarchy and the unique monarchy of the Pope, is precisely what another critic denies. For in what does the temporal power of the Papacy differ from the civil governments of the world except in the very elements which constitute it a theocracy.

"In a theocracy, God rules personally through man chosen by Himself, and is Himself the legislator. The Pope, unless you hold his temporal right to be adventitious, is chosen as temporal ruler by God, because he is already divinely chosen as priest and Pontiff. He is chosen as priest by a divine vocation, which is the personal and immediate action of God. He is constituted spiritual ruler by the positive and divine legislation of Christ. For neither in the old Israel, nor in the new, 'doth any man take honour to himself, but he that is called by God, as Aaron was.' Two divine elections from two distinct families were necessary, it is true, under the ancient theocracy, because Israel was constituted under dual tribal rights. Under the theocracy of the God-incarnate, the Pontiff-king needs only the one election, as being heir of the united authority of Christ. Christ is legislator and responsible even in respect to the limited temporal rule. For having chosen the Pontiff both as spiritual and temporal ruler, He is responsible for his temporal administration, the whole spirit of which is in subservience to the interests of the Universal Church. ' P. K. Q.' delivers his own opinion, no doubt, under the ægis of a great name. I will yield to none in admiration for the great Cardinal, whose example and authority I have always quoted. But on a question still undefined by the Church, his Eminence's utterance is only the opinion of a theologian. And that opinion was uttered a quarter of a century ago, when the lesson of events had yet to be learned, and the protests of the Vicar of Christ were only beginning, and theologians had not considered all the bearings of the question. Rather would it be prudent to hearken to a quite recent declaration of the Pope's representative to the American Church, on occasion of the Catholic Centenary. Archbishop Satolli, speaking of the Holy Father, said: ' He doubts not that the Catholics of America . . . will labour to that end—that the Pope will once more reacquire that independence and liberty which by divine institution appertain to him as Sovereign Head of all the Church and representative of the person and authority of Christ. . . .' If the Pope's independence and liberty appertain to him by divine institution, Christ makes Himself responsible for their exercise. Hence Christ retains and rules over a temporal inheritance among the kingdoms of the earth, whilst his spiritual government extends to all nations. The name coined by Josephus as truly applies, therefore, to the new law as it did to the old."

The following letter on " The Temporal Inheritance of the Roman Church " closes the correspondence :—

" In a previous letter, taking my stand on the teaching of the Church, I indicated that the foundation of the Pontiff's territorial right is neither the necessity of the temporal power, nor any fortuitous growth of circumstances, nor the accidental gift of emperors or kings ; but that the Roman Pontiff holds his temporal right from a special dispensation or ruling of Divine Providence. From the teaching of the Church I will now pass to the inspired word, and reverently seek to elicit its testimony on the subject. It will be found that the Pontiff's temporal right has its root and foundation and title in the remote past, that it was translated from the old law to the new, and, in reply to criticism, that even its extent is ascertainable. I pledge myself to the following proposition which will supply collateral evidence to my thesis : *'God's unrepented gift of land to the ancestors of Christ is the Roman Pontiff's title to temporal power, and an equivalent for the land God gave to the seed of Abraham is the inheritance of the Mother and Mistress Christian Church.'*

" 1. Oh! but the land of Israel was only given until the coming of Christ, will perhaps be the first objection, although too unguarded to credit any serious person with. An ample reply will be found in the question : why ? and the invitation to prove it ; for the promise of land was never otherwise characterised but as 'an everlasting possession.'

" 2. The land of Israel, it may be urged, being subjugated and made a Roman province, and its people scattered, God's gift was undone by violence and usurpation. In reply, it may be pointed out·that the conquest and usurpation of the land of Israel were no argument for the cancelling of God's gift when the Assyrians and Greeks conquered the country. Had the Jews remained faithful, many roads towards Jerusalem were opened to them after they had been scattered by the Romans, just as one road was open to them from Babylon after the Captivity.

" 3. The land of Israel, it may be further urged, was necessary for the people of God as a nation to prepare the way for the coming of Christ. This being accomplished, the gift of God was no longer necessary and was cancelled. In reply to this objection it may be pointed out that territorial rights, with political independence, was no more necessary for the worship of God in Israel than in the Mother and Mistress Christian Church. The children of Jacob could have worshipped Jehovah with sacrificial rites as a province of some peaceful empire, which, unlike the government of the Pharaohs and that of most earthly kings, would never have obstructed the work of God. It is, at all events, conceivable in the abstract. You will say : ' It is practically inconceivable ;' when you are met with the rejoinder : ' It is also practically inconceivable that the Mother and Mistress Christian Church will not be obstructed in the work of God without political independence and a territorial right.' Therefore this argument for cancelling God's gift at the extinction of the Church of the Synagogue collapses.

"4. In any case someone may insist the infidelity of the Jews caused the land of Israel to be forfeited. In reply to this objection let it be borne in mind that Christ and the faithful remnant, which then constituted the Mother and Mistress Christian Church, were more important than the carnal majority. Why, then, should they be deprived for the sins of others ? Unless it be proved that the Mistress Christian Church would not thenceforth require territorial independence, there is no reason yet why we should suppose that God repented of His gift.

"And what is more to the point, the land of Israel was never promised to the carnal Israelites, who were constantly being weeded out, but to the true children of Abraham. ' For all are not Israelites that are of Israel ; neither are all they that are the seed of Abraham children ; but in Isaac shall thy seed be called. That is. to say, not they that are the children of the flesh are the children of God, but they that are the children of the promise are accounted for the seed.' The promise, then, 'to thy seed will I give this land,' extends to the children of the promise who are accounted for the seed. It would be difficult, nay, impossible, to realise that the

Christian world has not inherited an equivalent territorial advantage for the Mother and Mistress Christian Church to make the promise good. The promise, inclusive of land, was made before the law, and reaches beyond it, not being circumscribed by it. Or, to use the Apostle's expression : ' The law, which was made after 430 years, doth not disannul, to make the promise of no effect ; for if the inheritance be of the law, it is no more of promise, but God gave it to Abraham by promise.' And although the Mistress Christian Church is principal heiress of the Synagogue, all Christians may and should lay claim to a share in her territorial independence. ' If you be Christ's, then are you the seed of Abraham, *heirs according to the promise.*' Some mind may suggest the scruple: ' You are applying to a temporal inheritance words which refer to Christ and His spiritual kingdom.' The plain answer to which is : ' No distinction is made by the Apostle, and the inheritance of territorial right not being struck out of the New Covenant, comes in for the same guarantee of lasting vitality. But a more severe retort would not be uncalled for, for the divorce between the spiritual and temporal inheritance would constitute Christians no longer *' heirs according to the promise.'*

" No doubt Christ is both principal inheritance and principal heir. But just because Christ is principal heir, is the promise of land chiefly addressed to Him, to be transmitted by Him to His principal joint-heir in the Christian Church : ' To thy seed will I give this land ; ' ' He saith not : and to his seeds, as of many : but as of one, and to thy seed, which is Christ.'

" The principal heir to the land of Israel was, therefore, Christ ; but here the argument must stop, for we could hardly dwell upon the principal temporal heir without getting into the main contention of the thesis and into the thoughts of Palm Sunday ; without calling for the sceptre of Juda and the throne of David, and shouting what the stones would have cried out had there not been an intelligent crowd to perform the loyal duty.

" 5. A difficulty may still be felt by some minds : if the territorial right bestowed upon the Church of the Synagogue be equivalently handed over to the Christian Mistress Church, one should expect to meet with some scriptural intimation or record of so important a transaction. And there is none. Well, some minds might possibly expect from Christ an authentically drawn up document or voucher witnessing to the sale of the Vineyard of Israel and to the divorce of the Church of the Synagogue, and indicating what equivalent he had taken in exchange. They need not go away quite disconsolate. The voucher may be found at the beginning of the fiftieth chapter of Isaias. The language is that of Christ : ' What is this bill of the divorce of your mother, with which I have put her away ; or who is my creditor, to whom I sold you ? Behold you are sold for your iniquities, and for your wicked deeds have I put your mother away. Because I came, and there was not a man.'

"The reflective mind will no doubt discern the meaning of ' the divorce of your mother ' in the sentence. It cannot apply to the Old Covenant, which would have given place to the New in any case. It cannot apply to the law. For the law was either essential and permanent, which Christ came not to destroy, or it was typical and ceremonial and only required fulfilling. The same must be said of the priesthood and the sceptre typically constituted under dual tribal right, which would have been translated to the united authority of Christ, even though iniquity had not abounded. The divorce, then, had nothing in common with the translation of the law and the priesthood. What remained to divorce ? Just the earthly and human side of the Church of the Synagogue : the Vineyard of Israel, with its majority of faithless people, its territory, its seat of spiritual rule on Mount Moriah, and of political rule on Mount Zion. The Jews had been constituted by the gift of God a Church with territorial independence. Christ divorces them, so that they may not even become a secularised nation. But He divorces in order to espouse, and henceforth divorce shall be no more. Having translated to the centre of the Gentile world the law and the priesthood, which are of divine origin, He espouses a new Church with equal territorial dowry, with equal political independence, and with a faithful people to be, in exchange for Israel, the Mother and Mistress Christian Church.

" But the transaction is enshrined in a double metaphor. Besides being a divorce of the Jewish Church, it is also a sale. And he who sells gets an equivalent. But to whom did Christ sell Israel? To whom was due the God-forsaken nation? or, as it is better put : ' Who is my creditor?' It required only registering the question. He redeemed them from the Egyptian to make them heirs of the promised land. He never sold them to the Assyrian or Greek. But the Roman was his creditor. For Rome was predestined to be the heiress of the Synagogue; and the Roman power was only allowed to root up the Church of the old alliance in exchange for the loss of Rome. Rome became the new promised land of the Mistress Christian Church and the patrimony of her first Pontiff. Peter, a son of Abraham, in the spirit and in the flesh, Peter, a principal joint-heir of the promise, was the first Pontiff-king of the New Covenant under the order of Melchisedech.

" 6. Where remains the forlorn hope? I hold that Christ divorced and sold the inhabitants, but not the territory, therefore he obtained no territorial equivalent for the Christian Church. The condensed reply to which may be quoted from 2 Machabees v.: ' But God did not choose the people for the place's sake, but the place for the people's sake. And therefore the place also itself was made partaker of the evils of the people ; but afterwards shall communicate in the good things, and, as it was forsaken in the wrath of Almighty God, shall be exalted again with great glory, when the great Lord shall be reconciled.'

" My proposition, then, holds good. Should any person, however, deem my position not impregnable, he is welcome to effect an entrance by the weak point and turn me out. No one, of course, will suppose for a moment that any new demarcations are being advocated. The thesis points to the central and constant fact of the temporal power of the Pope as the embodiment of a God-given right. The States of the Church, as they have been in times of peace, are the normal equivalent. For God's providence hath interpreted the right of the Pontiff.

" In speaking of demarcations, however, a landmark may be saluted before we leave the subject of the land of the Vicar of Christ. It is the house of Christ : the Santa Casa. It also had its translation, if we believe a well authenticated miracle. Thou wast not sold, O holy house ; but translated to the new promised land.

" Will Catholics throughout the world rise in their moral strength to vindicate the Pontiff's right? No doubt, if they become distinctly cognisant of it. This question, then, is too important to be overlooked ; and should be studied with that love and attention which the interests at stake do certainly command."

THE TRANSLATION OF THE THEOCRACY.

WITH ITS SPIRITUAL AND TEMPORAL INHERITANCE, FROM JERUSALEM TO ROME.

"Therefore I say to you, that the Kingdom of God shall be taken from you, and shall be given to a nation yielding the fruits thereof."—ST. MATTHEW xxi. 43.

SOME months ago a pilgrimage left our English shores for a land once holy, and for Jerusalem, its capital. And what was the general impression of the pilgrims? It may be summed up in the words of the Bishop who was the spiritual leader of the pilgrimage : " They saw the contours of the country, and knew it was the same, though now it looked like a land under a curse, and they only here and there saw the hand of man bring forth what might be produced." Such was the impression of the pilgrims. I may inquire, how could it be otherwise? The first martyr of Christ in that land was heard to say, "that Jesus of Nazareth shall destroy this place " (Acts vi, 14). A sale and a divorce under the Divine hand had occurred, in which it was decreed that the place itself should be made partaker. I have quoted elsewhere the testimony of Holy Scripture in reference to this unique event. In the fiftieth chapter of Isaias we read the following language of Christ : " What is this bill of the divorce of your mother, with which I have put her away ; or who is my creditor, to whom I sold you? " And in the second Book of Machabees, chapter v.: " But God did not choose the people for the place's sake, but the place for the people's sake. And therefore the place also itself was made partaker of the evils of the people; but afterwards shall communicate in the good things, and, as it was forsaken in the wrath of Almighty God, shall be exalted again with great glory, when the great Lord shall be reconciled."

No wonder, then, if the once holy land looks God-forsaken! Here is a principle: the land is destined to be partaker of the fate of the people. This principle applies, therefore, as much to the times of Caiphas and Pilate, or to the times of Vespasian and Titus, as to the times of Antiochus, as much to the times of a temporary punishment as to the times of a permanent casting off. Therefore, another people being taken up for the Divine government instead of the Jews, another city is chosen instead of Jerusalem.

To-day, in continuation of a theme which has been before my mind for some years, I have undertaken to unfold the Scripture evidence relating to the *Translation of the Theocracy, or Divine Government, with its Inheritance, both Temporal and Spiritual, from Jerusalem to Rome.*

Before entering on the subject, I may be allowed to anticipate a possible objection. I may be asked: "Why don't you quote the testimony of theologians and of the Fathers as well as that of Holy Writ?"

I have only one excuse to plead, that such would be a great undertaking for which I have not sufficient leisure time. So far as I have read and remember their testimony in respect of the Pope's temporal independence, my interpretation is either authorised or not condemned by them. But when appealing to the testimony of theologians in favour of the temporal power of the High Priest of the New Law and of the political independence of Rome, the Jerusalem of the New Covenant, it should be borne in mind that they were never confronted with anything like the present opposition to the Pope's independence. For the present opposition is not merely the outcome of violence, or bad behaviour, on the part of Catholic rulers as in the past. It is now a matter of deep speculation before the whole world. It is a question taken up and discussed by doctrinaires and decided against the Church.

" My kingdom is not of this world," has been hypocriti-
cally quoted by the worst enemies of the Spiritual Power;
as though Christ meant anything more by this declaration,
than that His temporal power was not based on the gift
of men, nor on the accident of human suffrage, nor on
the conquest of arms, but a divine gift and a divine
inheritance. We cannot, therefore, expect that theologians, not foreseeing the denial of a great truth, should
have sought to defend it. We must not be surprised
even if they passed over Scripture evidence, which is
altogether in harmony with the Pontiff's temporal sovereignty, or still more a direct proof of it. Their interpretation of many passages quoted in this and the
previous theses is so far favourable that they see the
bearing of the text, or declare it to be mysterious, or
partially admit its conclusion, or, not admitting it, fail
to give a satisfactory explanation. The royal dignity of
Christ, for instance, so frequently and emphatically declared in Holy Scripture, is admitted by theologians and
traced as a hereditary right. Yet many hesitate to say
that He really possessed the dignity or exercised the
right. Again, when commenting on the association of
Peter with Christ in the exemption from tribute, some
put it down to the poverty of the Divine Master ; whilst
others, with more reason, admit its significance, declaring
the privilege to be granted to Peter alone, because he
alone was heir to the plenitude of authority which Christ
left to his Church. When commenting on the words of
Christ and the Apostles recorded by St. Luke (xxii. 36,
38) : " 'And he that hath not, let him sell his coat, and
buy a sword ;' " and " ' Lord, behold here are two swords.'
And He said to them: ' It is enough'"—some hold that the
passage is mysterious, others explain it of the spiritual
and temporal swords, which both belong to the Church.
Yet if Christ were truly King, with an inalienable right
to be defended by his servants, what more natural than
this public exhibition of right before yielding it in
sacrifice. And if, as proved elsewhere, Peter was as-

sociated with Christ in both temporal and spiritual supremacy, what more natural than the reply of the Divine
Master in reference to the two typical swords : " It is
enough " ?

Take again the passage in the Acts of the Apostles,
(i. 6) : " ' Lord, wilt Thou at this time restore again
the kingdom to Israel ? ' But He said to them : ' It
is not for you to know the times or moments which the
Father hath put in His own power.' "

Here is a passage fully bearing on the kingly character of the Vicar and heir of Christ, and on the political
independence of Rome, the Jerusalem of the New
Covenant. The times or moments were known to the
Father, and fixed by His own power. By a merciful
dispensation, the eyes of the Apostles were closed on the
future. Only after a lapse of three centuries of bloody
persecution should the restoration come, and then not at
Jerusalem, but at Rome.

The passage, however, is interpreted by some as
though no temporal kingdom should belong to the
Church. The question of both Apostles and disciples
is ascribed to a want of spiritual-mindedness on their
part. The unwillingness of Christ to uplift the veil
which screened the future to a wish not to offend
their carnal nature and susceptibilities.

But as Christ, in necessarily alluding to " the times
and moments which the Father had put in His own
power," far from excluding, evidently grants and includes
in his reply the fact of the restoration of the kingdom to
Israel, the commentator is driven to adduce the spiritual
restoration of the Jews, who are to be united to the
kingdom of the Church at the end of the world. This
is an instance of a theologian wrestling with the obvious
meaning of a text, for want of having learned, as we
have, the necessity of the " Civil Principality " and the
law of invariable restoration by Divine Providence of the
temporal kingdom to the Roman Church, which holds
the place of Israel.

Take another instance, namely, the interpretation put upon the words of the Archangel to the Virgin Mary : "The Lord God shall give unto Him the throne of David his father, and He shall reign in the house of Jacob for ever." Here, again, from not distinguishing between the spiritual kingdom of the Church throughout the world and the political independence of the Pontiff in Rome, commentators have been driven to convert the throne of David into a spiritual one. But the chair of Moses was the spiritual throne. If it had been intended by God that Christ should inherit for the Church only a spiritual throne, the succession to the chair of Moses should have been pledged : "The Lord God shall give unto him the chair of Moses, and He shall reign in the house of Jacob for ever." But no, it is the throne of David, his father, a distinctly temporal and royal throne, which is pledged to the Church. Therefore we must perforce conclude, that behind His Vicar on that throne, both temporal and spiritual, "Christ shall reign in the house of Jacob for ever."

Without further preamble I hasten now to quote the text on which I trust to engage your kind and religious attention. It is the parable of the vineyard proposed by Isaias, completed by Christ, and recorded by St. Matthew, St. Mark, and St. Luke. The following is from St. Matthew xxi. 33: "'There was a man, a householder, who planted a vineyard, and made a hedge round about it, and dug in it a press, and built a tower, and let it out to husbandmen : and went into a strange country. And when the time of the fruits drew nigh, he sent his servants to the husbandmen, that they might receive the fruits thereof. And the husbandmen laying hands on his servants, beat one, and killed another, and stoned another. Again he sent other servants, more than the former : and they did to them in like manner. And last of all he sent to them his son, saying: "They will reverence my son." But the husbandmen, seeing the son, said among themselves : "This is the heir ; come, let us

kill him, and we shall have his inheritance." And taking
him, they cast him forth out of the vineyard, and killed
him. When, therefore, the lord of the vineyard shall
come, what will he do to those husbandmen ?' They say
to Him : ' He will bring those evil men to an evil end;
and he will let out his vineyard to other husbandmen,
that shall render him the fruit in due season.' Jesus saith
to them : 'Have you never read in the Scriptures : "The
stone which the builders rejected, the same is become
the head of the corner ? By the Lord this has been
done, and it is wonderful in our eyes." Therefore I
say to you, that the kingdom of God shall be taken from
you, and shall be given to a nation yielding the fruits
thereof. And whosoever shall fall on this stone, shall
be broken: but on whomsoever it shall fall, it shall grind
him to powder.' "

My commentary on this parable may be summed up
in the following argument :—

1. The parable in St. Matthew, chapter xxi., represents the theocracy with its spiritual and temporal
inheritance.

2. But the kingdom of God, which Christ foretold,
should be taken from the Jews, and should be given
to a nation yielding the fruits thereof, is identical with
the theocracy and inheritance depicted in the parable.

3. Therefore the theocracy, with its full inheritance,
spiritual and temporal, was, in fulfilment of Divine prophecy, taken from the Jews and given to a nation yielding the fruits thereof.

4. The nation which eventually inherited the theocracy, or kingdom of God, yielding the fruits thereof, can
only be the nation which is privileged to possess the
heir of Him Whom they killed.

5. Now according to Catholic teaching that nation
is Rome, etc.

6. Therefore Rome is the nation which eventually
inherited the theocracy. Therefore the theocracy, with
its temporal inheritance, was translated from Jerusalem
to Rome.

1. THE PARABLE IN ST. MATTHEW, CHAPTER XXI.,
   REPRESENTS THE THEOCRACY WITH ITS SPIRITUAL
   AND TEMPORAL INHERITANCE.

Isaias had applied the parable to Israel ; Christ
applies it also to the rulers of the nation, to the authorities of the Church, of the Synagogue, and to Himself.
The ownership of God and the Divine government,
together with the spiritual and temporal elements of
human government, are vividly pourtrayed in the parable
and we find them side by side in the history of Israel.
" The vineyard of the Lord of Hosts is the house of
Israel," says Isaias. The hedge made round about it is
understood by some to represent the protection afforded
. by the law, by others to represent the Divine protection. The press dug in it represents the Temple with its
altars. The tower, according to some, is the royal
dignity, which I may interpret as the temporal power.
The husbandmen are the chief citizens and those entrusted with power in this Church-nation. The servants
sent to the husbandmen to receive the fruits of the
vineyard are the prophets and the precursor. The son
sent at last represents Christ, Whom the Jews know to
be the heir, and consequently resolve to kill, that they
may secure the inheritance.

In one word, the parable is intended to give an
outline of the Jewish people and Jewish constitution.
Not only was the law divinely given, and the territory
divinely chosen, and the succession of priests and kings
divinely appointed, but the people also was divinely set
apart from the beginning to be a Church and a nation.
For as the householder planted the vineyard, so did God
from the beginning establish Israel. Moses was com-
manded to say : " You have seen what I have done to
the Egyptians, how I have carried you upon the wings
of eagles, and have taken you to Myself. If, therefore,
you will hear My voice, and keep My covenant, you shall
be *My peculiar possession* above all people : for all the

earth is Mine. And you shall be to Me *a priestly kingdom*, and a holy nation " (Exodus xix. 4-6).

Other nations were settled in their territory before the law-giver defined the sphere of religion or the limits of the spiritual power. The Israelites were set free and made a nation by God and religion. In other nations the secular power was predominant. In Israel the Church itself was the nation. Neither the spiritual power of the Jewish pontiffs nor the temporal power of the Jewish kings was subordinate. The spiritual and temporal powers had the same divine origin. They were supreme within their own respective spheres and coordinate. And whether king reigned or priest governed God held the sovereign sway. Hence Israel was unlike any other nation, a Church with political independence, or a Church-nation and a theocracy.

Now in thus planting Israel from the beginning, God had one only thing in view : to prepare the way for the Incarnation of His Divine Son, Who in the parable is represented as the heir.

It will be seen, therefore, that a temporal inheritance, as well as a spiritual one, was a preparation for the Incarnation of the Son of God. It is obvious also from the parable that the Jews sought to frustrate the Divine plan, by killing the heir and annihilating the theocracy, at the very time of its predestined perfection. " This is the heir, come, let us kill !him, and we shall have the inheritance." By these words of the parable, which Christ puts into the mouth of his enemies, He manifestly implies that they understood Him to be the heir. It might be interesting to examine the evidence which forced them to the conclusion that He was the heir. It will suffice, however, to consider in what sense they understood Him to be the heir. At the first glance we may safely judge that they knew Him to be a temporal as well as a spiritual heir. For the spiritual inheritance they had no care, except inasmuch as it might serve their carnal ends. They had corrupted their traditions and were seeking to establish themselves as a godless nation. Hence the temporal inheritance was the sole object of their jealous care, to preserve which they did not hesitate to do away with Him Whom the law and the prophets indicated as the heir of the Church-nation. The parable implies manifestly that the Jews understood that whatever authority existed in the nation was His. The vineyard was His. His was the protecting hedge, and the press dug in the vineyard. His was the tower, and to Him and to His Father belonged the servants that, in the long past, they had beaten or stoned or killed. They understood Him therefore to be the heir to the chair of Moses and to the throne of David, to be the heir of the kings, and of the priests, and of the prophets, and of Moses himself. Nay more, He had proved Himself in their presence to be the heir of God His Father. God, having ever shared with man the government of Israel, the inheritance was divine as well as human, and He was the God-man. It was temporal and spiritual, and they learned at last that he was born King of the Jews, and priest according to the order of Melchisedech.

In how many minds there remained crass ignorance, after the three years of Christ's public ministry, and in how many minds there was affected ignorance, the last day alone will reveal. One certain conclusion must be drawn from the parable, namely, that the leading portion of the nation knew Christ to be the heir of the theocracy, and of its spiritual and temporal inheritance. They knew it before the recitation of the parable. They had questioned His authority in Israel, and He informs them in reply that they were fully aware of His title and claims. He informs them that He also was aware of their murderous design.

The parable in St. Matthew, chapter xxi., is therefore a vivid representation of the theocracy, with its spiritual and temporal inheritance, at the time when the Heir appeared who could and did lay claim to its full inheritance, human and divine.

2. BUT THE KINGDOM OF GOD, WHICH CHRIST FORETOLD SHOULD BE TAKEN FROM THE JEWS, AND SHOULD BE GIVEN TO A NATION YIELDING THE FRUITS THEREOF, IS IDENTICAL WITH THE THEOCRACY AND INHERITANCE DEPICTED IN THE PARABLE.

By putting the case of the Jews in the form of a parable Christ had elicited their opinion that justice required an eviction and a change of hands. "They say to Him : ' He will bring those evil men to an evil end ; and will let out his vineyard to other husbandmen, that shall render him the fruit in due season.' " He now confirms their opinion, and shows them that they are themselves concerned, first by an appeal to Scripture : "The stone which the builders rejected, the same is become the head of the corner ;" and, secondly, by His own prophetic declaration : "Therefore I say to you, that the kingdom of God shall be taken from you, and shall be given to a nation yielding the fruits thereof." This record of the decreed translation of the kingdom of God to another nation is only to be found in St. Matthew. Elsewhere is recorded the judgment of the chief priests and ancients of the people in the case proposed in the parable, together with their discovery that it applied to them. Here Christ leaves the parable to come to what the parable means. Here He ceases to speak of the vineyard and inheritance to make a declaration in agreement with the Jews concerning that which the vineyard and inheritance signify, namely, the kingdom of God. Here He drops the figure of a first and second set of husbandmen to speak of the Jews themselves and of another nation destined to yield the fruits of the kingdom of God.

He reasons thus with the Jews: "You agree that the lord of the vineyard will let it out to other husbandmen that shall render him the fruit in due season. That vineyard is the inheritance that belonged to you. By your own showing, it should be taken from you. Therefore, the kingdom of God shall be taken from you. You shall be deprived of God's ownership and government so as to cease to be His *peculiar possession.* You shall be deprived of the Divine protection. You shall be deprived of the spiritual inheritance of God's service and of the temporal inheritance which made you a nation. And that which shall be taken from you shall be given to a nation yielding the proper fruits."

It is clear, therefore, that, in speaking of the kingdom of God in this place, Christ means the inheritance of Israel pourtrayed in the parable. And as God had His share in that inheritance as well as priest, king, and people, it is likewise clear that the kingdom of God is here meant for the theocracy with its spiritual and temporal inheritance.

3. THEREFORE THE THEOCRACY, WITH ITS FULL INHERI-
   TANCE, SPIRITUAL AND TEMPORAL, WAS, IN FULFIL-
   MENT OF DIVINE PROPHECY, TAKEN FROM THE JEWS
   AND GIVEN TO A NATION YIELDING THE FRUITS
   THEREOF.

If the two foregoing propositions are true, this last one follows of necessity. It is not, therefore, here necessary to set about proving it. It may be noted, however, that the kingdom of God represented in the parable, being a temporal as well as a spiritual kingdom, is not meant merely for the spiritual kingdom of the Universal Church, nor for the inheritance of the Faith among the Gentiles—I use the word merely because the theocracy of the God Incarnate is both a limited temporal kingdom and a universal spiritual one. The kingdom of God is none the less spiritual, and relates none the less to souls, and to Heaven hereafter, because the Incarnate God retains the temporal inheritance which was prepared for Him of old.

This conclusion receives a powerful confirmation from the words made use of by Christ. In speaking of the translation of the inheritance of Israel He might have said : " The kingdom of God shall be given to others," whereas He says : "shall be given to a nation yielding the fruits thereof." These words leave no doubt about the succession. It is one nation succeeding to the privileges of another nation that we have to go in search for.

Had Christ, on the other hand, said: "The kingdom of God shall be taken from you and given to the nations," we might have been puzzled at the alternative of the Jews retaining the monopoly of true religion in the world had they remained faithful, or at the other alternative of the Gentiles only receiving the Faith on account of the transgression of Israel ; but still we should have understood a spiritual inheritance. For a spiritual inheritance can extend throughout the world, whereas the temporal inheritance is limited in extent and must be confined to one people.

We should in such case have speculated in vain on the fate of the temporal inheritance of Israel. Perhaps forgetting, as some have done, that the Jews can never re-establish themselves on the old footing of the Mosaic law for want of genealogies, we might have concluded that the land of Israel, through pious remembrance called the Holy Land, still belonged to the Jews, who are destined to flourish there again before the end comes.

But we have not to speculate on the cancelling of God's temporal gift to Israel, nor on the breakdown of the kingdom of God. " The kingdom of God shall be taken from you, and shall be given to a nation yielding the fruits thereof." That is, shall be given to the Church which is fitted to be, instead of Israel, the Mistress Christian Church.

Reason and common sense bear out this interpretation. You must believe " the kingdom of God given to a nation yielding the fruits thereof " to be the theocracy with its temporal inheritance ; or you must believe that the Jews were destined, if they had been faithful, to retain a monopoly of the true Faith.

Had Christ in His mercy been able to gather the Jews, as the hen doth gather her chickens under her wings, what, then, would have happened? Surely, such repentance of the Jewish people would not have been fatal to the Gentiles! Yet in such an hypothesis the kingdom of God would not have been given to another nation. Therefore, the kingdom of God is not here identical with the inheritance of the Faith.

If you insist that it is, you must, perforce, conclude that such Faith would have remained with the repentant Jews, and would not have been given to another nation; and consequently that the conversion of the Jews to Christ would have been fatal to the Gentiles, which is absurd.

Therefore, it is once more proved that the theocracy, with its full inheritance, spiritual and temporal, was in fulfilment of Divine prophecy taken from the Jews and given to a nation yielding the fruits thereof.

4. THE NATION WHICH EVENTUALLY INHERITED THE THEOCRACY, OR KINGDOM OF GOD, YIELDING THE FRUITS THEREOF, CAN ONLY BE THE NATION WHICH IS PRIVILEGED TO POSSESS THE HEIR OF HIM WHOM THEY KILLED.

In order to discover the nation which hath succeeded to Israel by inheriting from Christ the kingdom of God, we must look out, not for a twofold dynasty of priests and kings, as under the old law, but for the heir of Christ, Who translated to Himself both the law and the priesthood, and united in His Person the whole authority of the ancient theocracy. Where that heir is at home, there shall the inheritance be, and there, consequently, the kingdom of God, or the theocracy.

Now in the natural order of things Jerusalem should have been the home of the heir of Christ, because in the normal state the theocracy should have remained in Israel. The Jews were entitled, if they had been willing to be gathered to the forgiving heart of the

Redeemer, to remain His principal inheritance. From Jerusalem the Faith would have continued to spread throughout the world for all time. Christians would have been named after Israel, their centre, and not after Rome. The theocracy established by God through Moses, without leaving its ancient home, would have received, and continued to hold, its predestined perfection in the Incarnation, which combines in one person the twofold authority of Pontiff and King. The order of Aaron and succession to the sceptre of Judah having reached their appointed goal, would have been merged into the order of Christ typified by Melchisedech.

But the natural order of things was not destined to endure. A violent act removed the theocracy to another 'centre. It was the cutting down of the natural branches of the olive tree to graft on the wild olive, and make it produce not the wild, but the original fruit. Whereas the wild tree should have been cut down, and should have received the graft from the old cultivated stock. It was the divorce and sale recorded by Isaias, followed by a fresh marriage with equal rights. It was the rejection of the stone by the Jewish builders, which became elsewhere the head of the corner.

And where was the theocracy removed to? Let us look for the heir of Christ. Once more, where he is at home there is the inheritance.

5. Now ACCORDING TO CATHOLIC TEACHING THE NATION WHICH IS PRIVILEGED TO POSSESS THE HEIR OF HIM WHOM THEY KILLED IS ROME.

We all hold that the Vicar of Christ is the heir to the plenitude of authority which He left to His Church. And that Rome, the Apostolic See, belongs to him. The only difficulty which besets some minds is the temporal inheritance of the old theocracy. Considering that the theocracy, as we have seen from Christ's words showing the application of the parable, was given to another nation, and that such other nation can only be Rome, it follows that Rome hath inherited the temporal inheritance of the theocracy. For the whole theocracy was handed over, and not merely a part of it. Christ, however, makes the light of the parable twice vivid by coupling with it another illustration, namely, that of the corner-stone rejected by the Jewish builders.

If the stone, which was the God Incarnate, heir of the theocracy, had not been rejected by the builders, it would have remained planted in Jerusalem. Peter and his successors, who are associated by inheritance in the firmness of that corner-stone, on which the Christian Church is built, would have remained in Jerusalem. Who, then, will venture to say that if the theocracy had thus remained in Israel, the temporal inheritance would have been forfeited? Who is prepared to assert that the Jewish Church would have been placed in a less favourable position for becoming the Mistress Christian Church? Or that political independence would not have been as much her birthright after as before the Incarnation? Or does the translation of the spiritual power of the theocracy to Rome involve the loss of the temporal inheritance? If the temporal inheritance had legitimately been conserved to a Mistress Christian Church in Jerusalem, why not to the heiress of the Church of Jerusalem? If the spiritual inheritance could be translated to Rome, why not the temporal inheritance?

In any case, no other nation claims, like Rome, to possess the heir of Him Whom they killed, neither do Catholics look elsewhere for the direct succession to Christ.

6. THEREFORE ROME IS THE NATION WHICH EVENTUALLY INHERITED THE THEOCRACY, OR KINGDOM OF GOD, YIELDING THE FRUITS THEREOF.

Schismatics in the East and in the West, to whom Rome is not the Jerusalem of the New Covenant, have fallen off the very foundation of religion, which is the unbroken succession of God's central and personal government in the world. A government which begins with the patriarchs and Abraham, "heir of the world " (Romans iv.), and extends to the reigning Roman Pontiff. Therefore, finally, the theocracy being handed over to another nation, and no other nation being privileged to possess the heir of Christ but Rome, it follows that *the theocracy, with its temporal inheritance, was translated from Jerusalem to Rome.*

THE NON-DESTRUCTION OF THE LAW OF ISRAEL.

We have seen in the foregoing thesis that the theocracy, the only everlasting kingdom on the earth according to the prophets, did not come to an end with the casting off of the Jewish people and of their ancient home in Israel. It has been shown that the Divine government, together with the priestly and kingly human rule, were translated to Christ and to the new order introduced by Him, and that the transference of such Divine and human government to another centre, Rome, was according to the Divine plan.

But government, whether human or divine, presupposes a legislation. We might conclude, therefore, without going further afield, that the law of Israel did not come to naught any more than the authority and legal powers established by it ; and, consequently, that what is termed the new law and the law of grace is only the fulfilment of the old by the heir of the theocracy.

It may be interesting, however, to attempt a short analysis of the Scripture evidence relating to the non-destruction of the law of Moses. We read in St. Matthew, ever the most faithful evangelist of the sacred humanity and royal dignity of Christ (chapter v. 17, *et seq.*) : " Do not think that I am come to destroy the law, or the prophets. I am not come to destroy, but to fulfil. For amen I say unto you, till Heaven and earth pass, one jot, or one tittle shall not pass of the law, till all be fulfilled. He, therefore, that shall break one of these least commandments, and shall so teach men, shall be called the least in the kingdom of Heaven," etc.

Here it should be observed that the law of Moses enjoined obedience, not only to the moral precepts, but to the authorities, divine and human, spiritual and temporal, constituted by the law. Therefore the words above quoted apply not only to the removal of certain dispensations, and to the perfect observance of the moral law, but to the recognition of the constituted authorities. Hence it was a public duty to acknowledge the Lord of Hosts as protector of Israel. It was a duty to pay tithes and acknowledge the authority of Levites and priests, a duty to acknowledge the authority of the succession of kings appointed by God, and it was the sin of rebellion or schism to break away from such authority. It will be seen, therefore, that if the law was not destroyed, but fulfilled, by Christ, so it fared with the theocracy.

It may be objected that Christ, in the passage just quoted, is speaking of the natural law and not of the law of Moses. If this were so, as indeed some commentators declare, it would be vain to seek a confirmation of the thesis from the words of Christ : " I am not come to destroy, but to fulfil."

But a little reflection will enable us to see that the declaration of Christ refers to the Mosaic law and not to the natural law. In the first place, Christ in the same breath makes an identical declaration in respect to the prophets. He would not have put the natural law in juxtaposition with the prophets, but the positive Divine law given through Moses, which, together with the prophets, were the interpretation of God's will and special designs in respect to His chosen people. Secondly, the supposition that Christ meant " I am not come to destroy the natural law," is absurd. The natural law, according to St. Thomas, is a participation of the eternal law by the rational creature. Christ could not be suspected, by friend or foe, of any intention of destroying it. Those who did not believe Him to be the Son of God, could at least infer the absence of such intention from His holy life and doctrine. Those who believed Him to be God, believed Him therefore to be the author of the natural law. And to say that " He came to fulfil the natural law" is also absurd, for the natural law had no reference to His coming and could not be fulfilled in that sense ; whereas the Mosaic law and the prophets were to be fulfilled by His coming. In the third place, the Jews to whom Christ spoke were not anxious about the natural law, which applies to all nations and to all men, but about their own law. It was quite natural, then, to seek to remove their apprehensions. The fulfilling of the law of Moses by Christ might seem in many respects a destroying. Christ declares that He came only to fulfil. Many dispensations had been granted under the old law, which though imperfect in respect to the law of Christ, was perfect for the time and people, as being God's own interpretation of the natural law. The withdrawal by Christ of such dispensations was not a destroying, but a fulfilling of the ancient law. The Jews had not been taught forgiveness of enemies, but mere justice and strict retribution. They knew not the perfection of indissoluble marriage, nor of monogamy, nor of celibacy. The removal of the relative imperfections of the law was not a destruction of the law. Not only the repeal of certain dispensations, but the fulfilling of all types and figures might appear to the Jews fatal to the law. Therefore Christ had to prepare the faithful Israelites for the cessation of the ceremonial law, with its typical sacrifices, and to warn them that in supplying the reality, He destroyed not the law, but merely that which was preliminary in the law.

Therefore, when declaring that He came not to destroy the law and the prophets, but to fulfil, Christ meant not the natural law, but the law of Moses. Therefore the law of Moses is fulfilled, and still endures in the law of Christ. Therefore the non-destruction by Christ of the law of Moses leaves intact that which was permanently established by such law, namely, the theo-cracy and its spiritual and temporal power. The theocracy, the most remarkable provision of the law of Moses, was not in itself of a preliminary or typical character ; there-fore it was not destroyed at the coming of the heir. Yet the form given to it by Moses was typical and indicative of imperfection. The delegated authority of the theocracy was divided between priest and king, and, as shown elsewhere, such separation of the spiritual and temporal powers in the government of the Church-nation could only be a type of the imperfection of the theo-cracy before the Son of God assumed a body and soul in the mystery of the Incarnation. It should be borne in mind that the human government of the theocracy has ever stood alone. It is like no other government that history describes. The two powers in Israel were co-ordinate and supreme. Before the Incarnation it was lawful for kings to hold spiritual authority and to be the high priests of the nation. But not in Israel. Since the Incarnation the very reverse is the law. Only in the theocracy of Rome are the spiritual and temporal powers combined. No other Christian king may hold spiritual power. The reason is that before the Incarnation the nations were not called together, but since the Incarna-tion the peoples of the world are assembled into one Church. They could not be assembled if they had more than one spiritual ruler ; and that spiritual ruler is the heir of the delegated authority of the theocracy.

NOTE FOR ELEVENTH PAGE.

After the words " Never was a high priest saluted or recognised as king," I have, for the sake of accuracy, added the words " by the nation " in the French edition.

That the two dignities were to be kept apart, and reserved to the priestly and kingly families respectively, may be shown both from Holy Scripture and from Josephus :—

1. We gather from the author of the first book of Machabees (chapter xiv.) that the Asmoneans were elected by the Jews, to be, not their kings, but their princes and high priests until the coming of Christ. " The Jews and their priests had consented that he (Simon) should be their prince and high priest for ever, till there should arise a faithful prophet . . ." (verse 41). " And it pleased all the people to establish Simon, and to do according to these words " (verse 46).

2. That the royal dignity belonged exclusively to the descendants of David, Josephus bears the following testimony. When he describes how the high priest introduces Jehoash, whom the Queen Athaliah, a precursor of Herod, had sought to destroy with the whole house of David, he quotes the following words, addressed by Jehoiada to the priests and Levites and heads of tribes assembled for the purpose and sworn to observe secrecy and lend assistance : " This is your king, of that house which you know God hath foretold should reign over you for all time to come " (Book IX. chapter vii.)

3. That such royal dignity did not belong to the Asmoneans may be deduced also from the testimony of Josephus, who records how the diadem was usurped by Aristobulus : " When their father Hyrcanus was dead, the eldest son, Aristobulus, intending to change the government *into a kingdom*, for so he resolved to do, first of all put a diadem on his head, " four hundred eighty and one years and three months after the people had been delivered from the Babylonish slavery " (Book

XIII. chapter xi.) The historian then proceeds to detail the barbarous cruelty of the self-made king to his mother and brethren.

4. That the nation was conscious that the priestly race were not entitled to kingly rule, Josephus bears testimony later on in Book XIV. chapter iii. After the tyrannical reign of Alexander, and the more peaceful reign of Alexandra, Aristobulus and Hyrcanus, her sons, quarrel over the succession, and present themselves before Pompey to settle the dispute. The historian says : " He (Pompey) came from Pella to Damascus ; and there it was that he heard the causes of the Jews, and of their governors Hyrcanus and Aristobulus, who were at difference with one another, as *also of the nation against them both*, which did not desire to be under *kingly government*, because the form of government which they received from their forefathers was that of subjection to the priests of that God whom they worshipped ; and (they complained) that though these two *were of the posterity of the priests*, yet did they *seek to change the government* of their nation to another form in order to enslave them."

DECLARATION OF THE BISHOPS.

READ BY CARDINAL MATTEI, DEAN OF THE SACRED COLLEGE.

Beatissime Pater,

Ex quo Apostoli Jesu Christi sacro Pentecostes die Petro
Ecclesia Capiti in oratione adhærentes, Spiritum Sanctum acceperunt,
et divino ejus impulsu acti, cunctarum fere nationem viris in Urbe
sancta congregatis, unicuique sua lingua potentiam Dei mirabilem an-
nunciarunt, nunquam, ut credimus, ad hanc usque diem tot eorumdem
hæredes, iisdem recurrentibus solemniis, venerandum Petri Successorem,
orantem circumsteterunt, decernentem audierunt, regentem roborarunt.
Quemadmodum vero Apostolis media inter nascentis Ecclesiæ pericula
nil jucundius accidere potuit, quam divino Spiritu recens afflato assistere
primo Christi in terris Vicario ; ita nec nobis præsentes inter Ecclesiæ
sanctæ angustias, antiquius sanctiusve aliud esse potuit, quam quidquid
inest venerationis pietatisque erga Sanctitatem Tuam pectoribus nostris,
ad pedes Beatitudinis Tuæ deponere, simul et unanimiter declarare,
quanta prosequamur admiratione præclaras, quibus Supremus Pontifex
Noster eminet virtutes, quantoque animo iis quæ Petrus alter docuit, vel
quæ tam firmiter stata rataque esse voluit, adhæreamus.

Corda nostra novus inflammat ardor, vividior fidei lux mentem
illuminat, sanctior animam corripit amor. Linguas nostras flammis
illius sacri ignis vibrantes sentimus quæ Mariæ, cui assidebant Apostoli,
mitissimum cor ardentiori pro hominum salute desiderio incendebant,
ipsos vero Apostolos ad magnalia Dei prædicanda impellebant.

Plurimas igitur agentes Beatitudini Tuæ gratias, quod nos ad Pon-
tificium solium difficillimis hisce temporibus accurrere, Te afflictum
solari, nostrosque Tibi, cleri item ac populi nostræ curæ commissorum
animi sensus aperire permiseris, Tibi uno ore unaque mente acclama-
mus, omnia fausta, cuncta bona adprecantes. Vive diu, Sancte Pater,
valeque ad Catholicam regendam Ecclesiam. Perge, ut facis, eam tuo
robore tueri, tua prudentia dirigere, tuis exornare virtutibus. Præi nobis,
ut bonus Pastor, exemplo, oves et agnos cœlesti pabulo pasce, aquis
Sapientiæ cœlestis refice. Nam Tu sanæ doctrinæ nobis Magister, Tu
unitatis centrum, Tu populi lumen indeficiens a divina Sapientia præ-
paratum. Tu petra es, et ipsius Ecclesia fundamentum, contra quod
inferorum portæ nunquam prævalebunt. Te loquente, Petrum audi-
mus, Te decernente, Christo obtemperamus. Te miramur inter tantas
molestias totque procellas fronte serena et imperturbato animo sacri
muneris partibus fungentem, invictum et erectum.

Dum tamen justissima in his gloriandi nobis suppetunt argumenta, non possumus quin simul oculos ad tristia convertamus. Undequaque enim menti nostræ se sistunt immania eorum facinora, qui pulcherrimam Italiæ terram, cujus Tu, Beatissime Pater, columen es et decus, misere vastarunt ipsumque tuum et Sanctæ Sedis principatum, ex quo præclara quæque in civilem societatem veluti ex suo fonte dimanarunt, labefactare, ac funditus evertere connituntur. Nam neque perennia sæculorum jura, neque diuturna regiminis pacifica possessio, neque tandem fœdera totius Europæ auctoritate sancita et confirmata impedire potuerunt, quominus omnia susdeque verterentur, spretis legibus omnibus, quibus hactenus suffulta stabant imperia.

Sed ut ad nostra propius accedamus, Te, Beatissime Pater, iis provinciis, quarum ope, et dignitate Sanctæ Sedis, et totius Ecclesiæ administrationem æquissime providebatur, nefario usurpatorum hominum scelere, qui non habent *nisi velamen malitiæ libertatem*, spoliatum cernimus. Quorum iniquæ violentiæ cum Sanctitas Tua invictissimo animo obstiterit, plurimas et gratias, Catholicorum omnium nomine, censemus rependendas.

Civilem enim Sanctæ Sedis principatum ceu quiddam necessarium ac providente Deo manifeste institutum agnoscimus; nec declarare dubitamus, in præsenti rerum humanarum statu, ipsum hunc principatum civilem pro bono ac libero Ecclesiæ animarumve regimine omnino requiri. Oportebat sane totius Ecclesiæ Caput Romanum Pontificem nulli principi esse subjectum, imo nullius hospitem; sed in proprio dominio ac regno sedentem suimet juris esse, et in nobili, tranquilla, et almo libertate Catholicam Fidem tueri, ac propugnare, totamve regere ac gubernare christianam rempublicam.

Quis autem inficiari possit in hoc rerum humanorum, opinionum, institutionumque conflictu necessarium esse ut servetur extrema in Europa medius, tres inter veteris mundi continentes, quidam veluti sacer locus, et sedes augustissima, unde populis principibusque vicissim oriatur vox quædam magna potensque, vox nempe justitiæ et veritatis, nulli favens præ cæteris, nullius obsequens arbitrio, quam nec terrendo compescere, nec ullis artibus quisquam possit circumvenire?

Qui porro vel hac vice fieri potuisset, ut Ecclesiæ Antistites securi hoc ex toto orbe accurrerent cum Sanctitate Tua de rebus gravissimis acturi, si ex tot et tam diversis regionibus gentibusque confluentes, Principem aliquem invenissent his oris dominantem, qui vel Principes ipsorum in suspicione haberet, vel illis, suspectus ipse, adversaretur? Sua sunt etenim et christiano, et civi officia; haud quidem repugnantia inter se, sed diversa tamen; quæ adimpleri ab Episcopis quomodo possent, nisi perstaret Romæ civilis principatus, qualis est Pontificum, juris alieni omnino immunis, et centrum quodammodo universalis concordiæ, nihil ambitionis humanæ spirans, nihil pro terrena dominatione moliens?

Ad liberum ergo Pontificum Regem venimus liberi, Ecclesiæ rebus utpote Pastores, et patriæ utpote cives bene et æque consulentes, neque Pastorum, neque civium officia posthabentes.

Quæ cum ita sint, quisnam Principatum illum tam veterem, tanta auctoritate, at tanta necessitatis vi conditum, audeat impugnare? Cui, si vel jus illud humanum, in quo posita est principum securitas populorumque libertas attendatur, quænam alia potestas possit comparari? Quæ tam venerabilis et sancta? Quæ sive pristinis, sive recentioribus sæculis monarchia vel respublica juribus tam augustis, tam antiquis, tam inviolabilibus possit gloriari? Quæ omnia si semel in hac Sancta Sede despecta atque proculcata fuerint, quisnam vel princeps de regno, vel respublica de territorio possint esse securi? Ergo, Sanctissime Pater, pro religione quidem, sed et pro justitia, juribusque, quæ sunt inter gentes rerum humanarum fundamenta, contendis atque decertas.

Sed de hac tam gravi causa vix nos decet amplius verba proferre, qui Te de ipsa non tam disserentem quam docentem sæpe sæpius audivimus. Vox etenim Tua, quasi tuba sacerdotalis, toti orbi clangens proclamavit, quod "singulari prorsus divinæ Providentiæ consilio factum sit, ut Romanus Pontifex, quem Christus totius Ecclesiæ suæ Caput centrumque constituit, civilem assequeretur principatum;"* ab omnibus igitur nobis esse pro certissimo tenendum non fortuito hoc regimen temporale Sanctæ Sedi accessisse, sed ex speciali divina dispositione illi esse tributum, longave annorum serie, unanimi omnium regnorum et imperiorum consensu, ac pæne miraculo corroboratum et conservatum.

Alto pariter et solemni eloquio declarasti "Te civilem Romanæ Ecclesiæ Principatum ejusque temporales possessiones ac jura, quæ ad universum Catholicum orbem pertinent, integra et inviolata constanter tueri et servare velle; immo Sanctæ Sedis Principatus Beatique Petri patrimonii tutelam ad omnes Catholicos pertinere; Teque paratum esse animam potius ponere quam hanc Dei, Ecclesiæ, ac justitiæ causam ullo modo deserere."† Quibus præclaris verbis nos acclamantes ac plaudentes respondemus, nos Tecum et ad carcerem et ad mortem ire paratos esse; Teque humiliter rogamus, ut in hac constantia ac firmissimo proposito maneas immobilis, angelis et hominibus invicti animi et summæ virtutis spectaculum factus. Id etiam a Te postulat Christi Ecclesia, pro cujus feliciori regimine Romanis Pontificibus civilis principatus providentissime fuit attributus, quæque adeo sensit ejusdem tutelam ad ipsam pertinere, ut, Sede olim Apostolica vacante, gravissimis in angustiis, temporales Romanæ Ecclesiæ possessiones omnes Constantiensis Concilii Patres, uti ex publicis patet documentis, in unum administrarent; id postulant Christi fideles per omnes terrarum orbis regiones dispersi, qui libere ad Te venire, libereque conscientiæ suæ consulere gestiunt; id denique ipsa civilis deposcit societas, quæ ex tui regiminis subversione sua ipsa nutare sentit fundamenta.

Sed quid plura? Tu tandem aliquando scelestos homines et honorum ecclesiasticorum direptores justo judicio damnans omnia quæ

---

* Lit. Ap. xxxi mar., 1860, pp. 3, 5. Allocutio, xx jun. 1859, p. 6. Encycl. xix jun., 1860, p. 4. Allocutio, xvii dec., 1860.

† Epist. Encycl., xix jan., 1860.

patraverant "irrita et nulla" proclamasti ;* actus omnes ab iis inten-
tatos "illegitimos omnino et sacrilegos" esse decrevisti ; † ipsosque
talium facinorum reos pœnis et censuris ecclesiasticis obnoxios jure ac
merito declarasti.‡

Hos tam graves Tui oris sermones, tamve præclara gesta nostrum
est reverenter excipere, iisque plenum assensum renovare. Sicuti enim
corpus capiti, cui jungitur membrorum compagine unaque vita, in
omnibus condolet, ita nos Tecum consentire necesse est. Tibi in omni
tua hac acerbissima afflictione, sic conjungimur, ut quæ tibi pati con-
tingat, eadem et nos, amoris consensu, patiamur. Deum interea sup-
plices invocamus, ut tam iniquæ rerum perturbationi finem ponat,
Ecclesiamque Filii sui sponsam, tam misere expoliatam ac oppressam
pristino decori ac libertati restituat.

Sed mirum nobis non est tam acriter, et infense Sedis Apostolicæ
jura impeti et impugnari. Jam enim a pluribus annis, eo devenit non-
nullorum hominum insania, ut non amplius singulas Ecclesia doctrinas
rejicere, vel in dubium revocare conentur ; sed totam penitus veritatem
christianam, christianamque rempublicam funditus evertere sibi pro-
ponant. Hinc impiissima tentamina vanæ scientiæ, falsæque eruditionis
contra Sacrarum Litterarum doctrinas, ipsarumque inspirationem ; hinc
malesana sollicitudo juventutem Ecclesiæ matris tutelæ substractam
quibusvis sæculi erroribus, vel seclusa sæpius omni religiosa institutione,
imbuendi ; hinc novæ eæque perniciosissimæ de sociali, politico æque
ac religioso rerum ordine theoriæ, quæ impune quaquaversus spargun-
tur ; hinc multis familiare, in his præsertim oris, Ecclesiæ auctoritatem
spernere, jura sibi vindicare, præcepta proculcare, ministros vilipendere,
cultum deridere, ipsos de religione errores, imo ecclesiasticos quoque
viros in perditionis viam misere abeuntes laudare ac in honore habere.
Venerabiles Antistites ac Dei Sacerdotes exauctorantur, exulare coguntur, aut in carceres detruduntur ; quinimo ante tribunalia civilia, pro
constantia in sacro ministerio obeundo, contumeliose pertrahuntur.
Gemunt Christi Sponsæ suis expulsæ tectis, inediæ fere consumptæ, vel
cito consumendæ ; viri religiosi ad sæculum inviti remeare coguntur ;
sacro 'Ecclesiæ patrimonio violentæ manus injiciuntur ; pessimorum
librorum, ephemeridum, et imaginum colluvie, fidei, moribus, veritati,
ipsi verecundiæ continuum asperrimumque bellum infertur.

Sed qui talia moliuntur optime norunt in Sancta Sede, velut in arce
inexpugnabili, robur ac vires omnis veritatis ac justitiæ inesse, quibus
retundantur hostium impetus ; ibi esse speculam, ex qua vigiles Summi
Custodis oculi paratas insidias a longe conspiciunt, suis annuntiandas
commilitonibus. Hinc odium implacabile, hinc insanabilis livor, hinc
continuum scelestissimorum hominum studium, ut Sanctam Romanam
Ecclesiam ejusque Sedem deprimant, ac si fieri unquam posset, prorsus
exscindant.

* Allocutio, xxvi sept., 1859.
† Allocutio, xx jun. 1859.
‡ Litteræ Apostolicæ, xxvi martii, 1860.

Quis, Beatissime Pater, talia conspiciens, vel etiam recensita audiens sibi temperet a lacrymis ? Justo igitur dolore correpti oculos ac manus ad cœlos levamus, divinum illum Spiritum toto mentis affectu implorantes, ut qui hac die olim nascentem Ecclesiam sub Petri regimine sanctificavit et roboravit, eam nunc, Te pastore, Te duce, tuetur, ampliet, ac glorificet.

Testis sit votorum quæ nuncupamus, Maria per Te Immaculatæ titulo hoc ipso in loco solemniter aucta ; testes hi sacri cineres quos veneramur Sanctorum Romanæ Ecclesiæ Patronorum Petri et Pauli ; testes venerandæ exuviæ tot Pontificum, Martyrum, ac Confessorum, quæ hanc ipsam, quam premimus terram, sanctam reddunt ; testes tandem præcipue nobis adstent Sancti isti, qui Cœlitum Ordini hac ipsa die supremo Tuo judicio adscripti, hodie Ecclesiæ tutelam novo titulo sunt suscepturi, primasque Omnipotenti Deo preces pro Tua quoque incolumitate suis de altaribus oblaturi.

Adstantibus igitur istis omnibus, nos Episcopi, ne illud impietas vel ignorare simulet, vel audeat denegare, errores quos Tu damnasti, damnamus, doctrinas novas et peregrinas, quæ in damnum Ecclesiæ Jesu Christi passim propagantur, detestamur et rejicimus ; sacrilegia, rapinas, immunitatis ecclesiasticæ violationes, aliaque nefanda in Ecclesiam, Petrique Sedem commissa reprobamus, et condemnamus.

Hanc vero protestationem, quam publicis Ecclesiæ tabulis adscribi petimus, Fratrum etiam nostrorum qui absunt nomine, tuto proferimus ; sive eorum qui, tot inter angustias, vi detenti domi hodie silent ac plorant, sive qui gravibus negotiis, aut adversa valetudine impediti, nobiscum hodie adesse nequiverunt. Jungimus insuper nobis fidelem nostrum Clerum ac populum, qui eodem ac nos in Te amore, eadem pia reverentia animati, suum in Te studium, qua precibus sine intermissione fusis, qua opibus in Obolo S. Petri mira, ut plurimum, largitate oblatis lucentissime comprobarunt, probe scientes sacrificiis suis id quoque curari, ut dum necessitatibus Supremi Pastoris consulitur, simul et ejusdem libertati servandæ prospiciatur.

Utinam ad communem hanc totius Orbis christiani, imo omnis socialis ordinis causam in tuto locandam universi populi conspirarent !

Utinam intelligerent erudirenturque Reges et sæculi potestates, causam Pontificis omnium principum regnorumque esse causam, et quo tendant nefarii adversariorum ejus conatus, ac tandem *novissima providerent !*

Utinam resipiscerent infelices illi aliquot ecclesiastici et religiosi viri qui vocationis suæ immemores debitam Ecclesiæ Præsulibus obedientiam denegantes, atque ipsum quoque Ecclesiæ magisterium temere usurpantes, in viam perditionis abierunt !

Hoc a Domino Tecum flentes, Beatissime Pater, enixe atque ex corde exoramus dum ad Tuos sacros pedes provoluti, a Te robur cœleste expetimus, quod Apostolica ac Paterna Benedictio tua valet impertire. Sit hæc copiosa et ex intimis penetralibus Cordis Tui largiter effluens, ut non tantum nos, sed absentes quoque dilectissimos Fratres itemque Fideles nobis commissos irriget ac perfundat. Sit talis quæ nostros et totius Orbis dolores leniat et demulceat, infirmitatem sublevet, operam ac laborem fæcundet, feliciora demum Ecclesiæ Sanctæ Dei tempora acceleret.

Manus, card. MATTEI, évêque d'Ostie et de Velletri.
Constantinus, card. PATRIZI, évêque de Porto et de Sainte-Rufine.
Aloisius, card. AMAT, évêque de Preneste.
Antonius Maria, card. CAGIANO DE AZEVEDO, évêque de Tusculum.
Hieronymus, card. D'ANDREA, évêque de Sabine.
Ludovicus, card. ALTIERI, évêque d'Albano.
Engelbertus, card. STERSEX, archevêque de Malines
Ludovicus-Jacobus-Mauritius, card. de BONALD, archevêque de Lyon.
Fredericus-Joannes-Joseph, card. SCHWARZENBERG, archevêque de Prague.
Dominicus, card. CARAFA DE TRAETTO, archevêque de Benevent.
Xystus, card. RIARO SPORZA, archevêque de Naples.
Jacobus-Maria-Ant.-Cæsar, card. MATHIEU, archevêque de Besançon.
Thomas, card. GOUSSET, archevêque de Rheims.
Nicolaus, card. WISEMAN, archevêque de Westminster.
Franciscus-Augustus, card. DONNET, archevêque de Bordeaux.
Joannes, card. SCYTOWSKI, archevêque de Strigonie (Gran).
Franciscus-Nicolaus-Maddalena, card. MORLOT, archevêque de Paris.
Joseph-Maria, card. MILESI, abbé commend. et ordinaire des Trois-Fontaines.
Michael, card. GARCIA CUESTA, archevêque de Compostelle.
Cajetanus, card. BEDINI, évêque de Viterbe et Toscanella.
Ferdinandus, card. DE LA PUENTE, archevêque de Burgos.
Melchiades FERLIST, patriarche de Constantinople.
Catillus BELGRADO, patriarche d'Antioche.
Joseph TREVISANATO, patriarche de Venise.
Thomas IGLESIAS Y BARCONES, patriarche des Indes occidentales(Espagne).
Antonius HASSOUN, primat de Constantinople, du rite arménien.
Aloisius-Maria CARDELLI, archevêque d'Acrida (en Macédoine *in partibus*).
Stephanus MISSIR, archevêque d'Hiéranopolis, du rite grec (Irenopol, *in partibus*).
Laurentius TRIOCHE, archevêque de Babylone, du rite latin.
Tobias AUN, archevêque de Béryte des Maronites (Beyrouth).
Emmanuel MARONGUI NUREA, archevêque de Cagliari.
Joannes-Joseph-Maria DE JERPHANION archevêque d'Alby.
Joannes-Franc. COMETTI, archevêque de Nicomédie.
Melionus DE JOLLY, archevêque de Sens.
Leo DE PRZYLUSKI, archevêque de Gnesen et Posen.
Alexander AZINARI DE SANMARZANO, archevéque d'Ephèse.
Edoardus HURMUZ, archevêque de Sirac, du rite arménien.
Raphael D'AMROSIO, archevêque de Dyrrachium (Durazzo).
Joseph-Maria DEBELAY, archevêque d'Avignon.
Paulus CULLEN, archevéque de Dublin.
Thomas-Ludovicus CONNOLLY, archevêque d'Halifax.
Joannes-Baptista PURCELL, archevêque de Cincinnati.
Joannes HUGHES, archevêque de New-York.
Renatus-Franciscus REGNIER, archevêque de Cambrai.
Maximilianus DE TARNOCZY, archevêque de Salzbourg.
Antonius LIGI BUSSI, archevêque d'Iconium.

Aloisius CLEMENTI, archevêque de Damas.
Silvester GUEVARA, archevêque de Venezuela.
Joannes ZWYSEN, archevêque d'Utrecht.
Fredericus DE FURSTENBERG, archevêque d'Olmutz.
Paulus BRUNONI, archevêque de Taron *(in partibus)*, vicaire aposto-
lique, patriarche pour les Latins à Constantinople.
Athanasius SABUCH, archevêque de Tyr, Melchite.
Andreas BIZZARRI, archevêque de Philippes *(in partibus)*.
Franciscus-Xav. APUZZO, archevêque de Sorrente.
Andreas GOLLMAYR, archev. de Goritz et de Gradisca.
Vincentius TIZZANI, archevêque de Nisibe.
Petrus VILLANOVA CASTELLACCI, archevêque de Pétra.
Vincentius SPACCAPIETRA, archevêque de Smyrne.
Michael ALEXANDRIORUM, archevêque de Jérusalem, rite arménien.
Marianus RICCIARDI, archevêque de Reggio (en Calabre).
Salvator NOBILE VITELLESCHI, archevêque de Séleucie.
Alexander FRANCHI, archevêque de Thessalonique (Salonique).
Gregorius SCHERR, archevêque de Munich et Frisingue.
Georgius-Claudius-Ludovicus-Pius CHALANDON, archevêque d'Aix.
Joseph-Dominicus COSTA Y BORRAS, archevêque de Tarragone.
Ludovicus DE LA LASTRA Y CUESTA, archevêque de Valladolid.
Gustavus D'HOHENLOHE, archevêque d'Edesse.
Cajetanus PACE FORNO, archevêque de Rhodes, évêque de Malte.
Philippus GALLO, archevêque de Patras.
Petrus GIANELLI, archevêque de Sardes.
Emmanuel-Gargia GIL, archevêque de Saragosse.
Goffredus BROSSAIS SAINT-MARC, archevêque de Rennes.
Julianus-Florianus DESPREZ, archevêque de Toulouse.
Spiridion MADDALENA, archevêque de Corcyre (Corfou).
Marianus BARRIO Y FERNANDEZ, archevêque de Valence (en Espagne).
Franciscus-Augustus DELAMARRE, archevêque d'Auch.
Carolus DE LA TOUR-D'AUVERGNE, archevêque de Bourges.
MELETIOS, archevêque de Drama, rite grec.
Petrus-Dominicus MAUPAS, archevêque de Zara.
Ignatius GIUSTINIANI, évêque de Scio.
Raphael-Sanctes CASANELLI, évêque d'Ajaccio.
Ludovicus-Carolus FÉRON, évêque de Clermont.
Guillelmus SILLANI, ancien évêque de Terracine.
Nicolaus-Joseph DEHESSELLE, évêque de Namur.
Ignatius BOURGET, évêque de Marianopolis (Saut-Sainte-Marie).
Jacobus GILDIS, évêque de Lymira (vicaire apostolique à Edimbourg).
Fredericus-Gabriel DE MARGUERYE, évêque d'Autun.
Joseph MONTIERI, évêque de Ponte-Corvo.
Ludovicus DELEBECQUE, évêque de Gand.
Ludovicus BESI, évêque de Canope.
Georgius-Antonius STAHL, évêque de Wurzbourg.
Thomas-Joseph BROWN, évêque de Newport.
Carolus GIGLI, évêque de Tivoli.
Franciscus-Maria VIBERT, évêque de Maurienne.
Joannes Amatus DE VESINS, évêque d'Agen.
Joannes TOPICH, évêque de Philippopoli.
Nicolaus CRISPIGNI, évêque de Mandela (Poggio Mirteto).
Andreas RŒSS, évêque de Strasbourg.
Nicolaus WEISS, évêque de Spire.

Joseph-Armandus GIGNOUX, évêque de Beauvais, Noyon et Senlis.
Joannes-Baptista-Leonardus BERTEAUD, évêque de Tulle.
Joannes-Jacobus-David BARDOU, évêque de Cahors.
Guillelmus ARNOLDI, évêque de Trèves.
Joannes-Franciscus WEHLAND, évêque de la Nouvelle-Orléans.
Paulus-Georgius DUPONT DES LOGES, évêque de Metz.
Joannes-Bernardus FITZ-PATRICK, évêque de Boston.
Joannes MAC-CLOSKEY, évêque d'Albany.
Petrus SEVERINI, évêque de Sappa, en Albanie.
Joannes-Martinus HENNY, évêque de Milwaukie.
Joannes-Baptista ROSANI, évêque d'Ærythrée.
Joannes DONEY, évêque de Montauban.
Petrus-Joseph DE PREUX, évêque de Sion.
Gaspard BAROWKI, évêque de Zytomir.
Carolus MAC-NALLY, évêque de Clogher.
Bernardus-Maria TIRABASSI, évêque de Ferentine.
Urbanus BOGDANOVICH, évêque de Europo *(in partibus)*.
Jacobus-Maria-Joseph BAILLES, ancien évêque de Luçon.
Joannes-Baptista PELLEI, évêque d'Acquapendente.
Stephanus MARILLEY, évêque de Lausanne et Genève.
Theodorus-Augustinus FORCADE, évêque de Nevers.
Ludovicus-Antonius-August. PAVY, évêque d'Alger.
Antonius-Martinus SLOMSCHEK, évêque de Lavant.
Guillelmus-Bernardus ULLATHORNE, évêque de Birmingham.
Aloisius RICCI, évêque de Segni.
Joseph-August.-Victor DE MORLHON, évêque du Puy.
Joannes TIMON, évêque de Buffalo.
Amadeus RAPPE, évêque de Cleveland
Guillelmus KEANE, évêque de Cloyne. .
Joseph-Maria-Benedictus SERRA, évêque de Daulo.
Paulus DODMASSEI, évêque d'Alexia (Alessio, en Albanie).
Angelus PARSI, évêque de Nicopoli.
Joannes-Georgius MULLER, évêque de Munster.
Camilius BISLETI, évêque de Corneto et de Civita-Vecchia.
Joannes-Thomas MULLOCK, évêque de Saint-Jean de Terre-Neuve.
Dominicus CANUBIO Y ALBERTO, évêque de Segorbe.
.Joannes-Antonius BALMA, évêque de Ptolémaide (Sainte-Jean d'Acre), *in partibus.*
Aloisius KOBES, évêque de Metone, *in partibus*, vicaire apostolique d e la Guinée.
Julianus-Maria MEIRIEU, évêque de Digne.
Joannes-Anton.-Maria FOULQUIER, évêque de Mende.
Franciscus KELLY, évêque de Titopoli.
Antonius-Felix DUPANLOUP, évêque d'Orléans.
Joannes-Antonius BAUDRI, évêque d'Aréthuse, *in partibus*, suffragant de l'archeveque de Cologne.
Joannes RANOLDER, évêque de Vestprim (Hongrie).
Petrus-Simon-Ludov. DE DREUX-BREZE, évêque de Moulins.
Joseph ARACHIAL, évêque de Trébizonde, 1ite arménien.
Franciscus PETAGNA, évêque de Castellamare.
Guillelmus DE KETTELER, évêque de Mayence.
Antonius-Carolus COUSSEAU, évêque d'Angoulême.
Clemens MUNGUIA, évêque de Mechoacan.
Carolus-Franciscus BAILLARGEON, évêque de Thoa, *in partibus.*

Guillelmus TURNER, évêque de Salford
Mathias-Augustinus MENCACCI, évêque de Civita-Castellana.
Joannes-Petrus MABILE, évêque de Versailles.
Thomas GRANT, évêque de Southwark.
Caietanus BRINCIOTTI, évêque de Bagnorea.
Joannes-Bapt.-Paulus Maria LYONNET, évêque de Valence (en France).
Ignatius FEIRGELLE, évêque de Saint-Hippolyte (Saint-Pœlten).
Ludovicus RAYNALD, évêque de Transylvanie.
Joannes-Jacobus-Antonius GUERRIN, évêque de Langres.
Ludovicus-Eugénius REGNAULT, évêque de Chartres.
Joseph LAVOCQUE, évêque de Saint-Hyacinthe.
Joseph CARDONI, évêque de Carista.
Gesualdus VITALI, évêque d'Agathopolis, *in partibus*, suffragant de Velletri.
Laurentius BLANCHERI, évêque de Legione, *in partibus*.
Aloisius FILIPPI, évêque d'Aquila.
Joseph-Maria GINOULHIAC, évêque de Grenoble.
Franciscus-Joseph RUDIGER, évêque de Linz.
Joseph CAIHAL Y ESTRADE, évêque d'Urgel.
Joannes KILDUFF, évêque d'Ardagh.
Joannes LOUGHLIN, évêque de Brooklyn.
Joannes-Franciscus a Paula VEREA, évêque de Linarès (Mexique).
Jacobus ROOSEVELL-BAYLEY, évêque de Newark.
Petrus ESPINOSA, évêque de Guadalaxara.
Aloisius CIURCIA, évêque de Scodra (Scutari).
Ottocarus DE ATTEMS, évêque de Seckau.
Nicolaus BEDINI, évêque de Terracine.
Ludovicus-Maria-Joseph CAVEROT, évêque de Saint-Dié.
Hieronymus FERNANDEZ, évêque de Palenica.
David MORIARTY, évêque de Kerry.
Benedictus RICABONA, évêque de Trente.
Olympus-Philip GERBET, évêque de Perpignan.
Aloisius JONA, évêque de Montefiascone.
Petrus BARAJAS, évêque de Saint-Louis du Potosi.
David BACON, évêque de Portland.
Franciscus-Alexander ROULLET DE LA BOUILLERIE, évêque de Carcassonne.
Joannes-Joseph VITEZICA, évêque de Veglietz.
Cajetanus RODILOSSI, évêque d'Alatri.
Nicalaus-Renatus SERGENT, évêque de Quimper.
Pelagius-Antonius LAVASTIDA, évêque de Tlascala.
Guillelmus VAUGHAN, évêque de Plymouth.
Laurentius SIGNANA, évêque de Sutri et Népi.
Nicolaus PACE, évêque d'Améla.
Claudius-Henricus PLANTIER, evêque de Nimes.
Jacobus DUGGAN, évêque de Chicago.
Clemens SMITH, évêque de Dubuque.
Andreas CASASOLA, évêque de Concordia (Etats vénitiens).
Antonius-Joseph JORDANT, évêque de Fréjus et Toulon.
Laurentius GILLOOLY, évêque d'Elphin.
Daniel MAC-GETTIGAN, évêque de Raphoe.
Joannes DOLTON, évêque de Port-Grace (Harbour-Grace, Terre-Neuve).
Joannes FARRELL, évêque d'Hamilton.
Stephanus SEMERIA, évêque d'Olympe *in partibus*, vicaire apostolique
de Jafnapatam.
Carolus-Nicolaus DIDIOT, évêque de Bayeux.

Conradus MARTIN, évêque de Paderborn.
Joannes-Honoratus BARA, évêque de Châlons.
Joseph WIBER, évêque de Halia, *in partibus*, suffragant de l'archevêché de Strigonie (Gran).
Laurentius BERGERETTI, évêque de Santorin.
Michael MARSZWLKI, évêque de Wladislav.
Vincentius GASSER, évêque de Brixen (Bressano).
Franciscus MARINELLI, évêque de Porphyre.
Fortunatus MAURIZI, évêque de Veroli.
Fredericus-Jacobus WOOD, évêque de Philadelphie.
Joannes MAC-EVILEY, évêque de Galway.
Thomas FURLONG, évêque de Fernes.
Guilelmus-Joseph CLIFFORD, évêque de Clifton.
Petrus-Hendricus GERAUD DE LANGALERIE, évêque de Belley.
Ludovicus DELCUSY évêque de Viviers.
Joannes SIMOR, évêque de Giavarino.
Joannes-Bapt. SCANDEDLA, évêque d'Antinoé, vicaire apostolique de Gibraltar.
Paulus MELCHERS, évêque d'Osnabruck.
Petrus-Antonius DE POMPIGNAC, évêque de Saint-Flour.
Anastasius-Rodrigus YUNTO, évêque de Salamanque.
Joannes Ignatius MORENO, évêque d'Oviedo.
Antonius DOMINGUEZ Y VALDECAGNAS, évêque de Cadix.
Michael O'HEA, évêque de Ross.
Bernardus GONDE Y GORRAL, évêque de Plasencia.
Franciscus a Paula BENAVIDES, évêque de Siguenza.
Fernandinus BLANCO, évêque d'Avila.
Joannes-Joseph CASTANER Y RIVAS, évêque de Vich.
Cosmas MARRODAN Y RUBIO, évêque de Tarragone.
Mathæus JAUME Y GARUN, évêque de Minorque.
Petrus-Lucas ASSENSIO évêque de Jaca.
Joseph-Maria PAPARDO, évêque de Sinope.
Clemens PAGLIARI, évêque d'Anagni.
Franciscus MAC-FARLAND, évêque d'Hartford.
Franciscus LACROIX, évêque de Bayonne.
Ignatius SENESTRY, évêque de Ratisbonne.
Joannes-Sebast. DEVOUCOUX évêque d'Evreux.
Edoardus HOKAN, évêque de Kingston.
Franciscus-Kerril AMHERST, évêque de Northampton.
Paschalus VUIHIC, évêque d'Antiphelle, vicaire apostolique en Egypte.
Andreas ROSALES Y MUNOZ, évêque de Jaen.
Michael PAYA Y RICO, évêque de Cuença.
Petrus CUBERO Y LOPEZ DE PADILLA, évêque d'Orihuela.
Joannes-Antonius-Augustus BELAVAL, évêque de Pamiers.
Valentinus WIERY, évêque de Gurk.
Antonius HALAGI, évêque d'Artuin, rite arménien.
Joannes-Joseph LYNK, évêque de Toronto.
Joseph-Lopez CRESPO, évêque de Santander.
Ludovicus-Maria-Olivenus EDIVENT, évêque d'Aire.
Petrus-Jeremias-Michael-Angelus CELESIA, évêque de Patti.
Alexander-Paulus SPOGDIA, évêque de Ripatransone.
Joannes MONETTI, évêque de Cervia.
Petrus MAC-INTYRE, évêque de Charleston.
Michael DOMENEC, évêque de Pittsburg.

Alexander BONNAZ, évêque de Csanad et Temeswar
Darius BUCCIARELLI, évêque de Pulati (Turquie).
Gerardus-Petrus WILMER, évêque d'Harlem.
Georgius BUTLER, évêque de Sidonie, *in partibus*.
Patricius-Franciscus CRUISE, évêque de Marseille.
Joseph-Maria COVARUBIAS, évêque d'Antequera.
Robertus CORNTHWAITE, évêque de Beverley.
Aloisius DI CANOSA, évêque de Vérone.
Laurentius STUDACH, évêque d'Orthosie, vicaire apostolique de Suède et Norvège.
Joseph BERARDI, archevêque élu de Nicée.

www.ingramcontent.com/pod-product-compliance
Lightning Source LLC
Chambersburg PA
CBHW031452270326
41930CB00007B/969